D1562945

VOICES FROM THE BATTLEFRONT

Achieving Cultural Equity

Edited by Marta Moreno Vega
& Cheryll Y. Greene

A Caribbean Cultural Center Book

Africa World Press, Inc.

P.O. Box 1892
Trenton, New Jersey 08607

Africa World Press, Inc
P.O. Box 1892
Trenton, N.J. 08607

Copyright © The Caribbean Cultural Center 1993
First Printing 1993

Book Design by Jonathan Gullery
Book Cover Design & Illustration by George R. Smith

Library of Congress Cataloging-in-Publication Data

Voices from the battlefront : achieving cultural equity / edited by
    Marta Moreno Vega & Cheryll Y. Greene.
        p.   cm.
    ISBN 0-86543-393-3. -- ISBN 0-86543-394-1 (pbk.)
    1. Pluralism (Social sciences) -- United States. 2. Minorities-
    -United States. 3. Multiculturalism -- United States. 4. United
    States -- Race relations. 5. United States -- Ethnic relations.
    I. Vega, Marta Moreno. II. Greene, Cheryll Y.
    E184. A1V69   1993
    305.8 ' 00973--dc20   93 - 24658
                                        CIP

Conditioned by a changing world, classic norms of social analysis have been eroded since the late 1960s. . . . The shift in social thought has made questions of conflict, change, and inequality increasingly urgent. Analysts no longer seek out harmony and consensus to the exclusion of difference and inconsistency. For social analysis, cultural borderlands have moved from a marginal to a central place. In certain cases, such borders are literal. Cities throughout the world today increasingly include minorities defined by race, ethnicity, language, class, religion, and sexual orientation. Encounters with "difference" now pervade modern everyday life in urban settings.

Renato Rosaldo,
Culture and Truth:
The Remaking of Social Analysis

CONTENTS

Foreword ... ... *xi*
Molefi Kete Asante

Acknowledgments ... ... *xiii*

Introduction ... ... *xv*

I. Frameworks

Rethinking Who *We* Are:
A Basic Discussion of Basic Terms 3
John Kuo Wei Tchen

Afrocentricity: A Philosophical Basis
for Cultural Equity Battles? 11
Harold Cruse

Setting the Record Straight:
A View from Seneca Country 23
G. Peter Jemison

Appalachia, Democracy, and Cultural Equity 31
Dudley Cocke

Indigenismo: The Call to Unity 41
Amalia Mesa-Bains

II. Battle Stances

"Battle Stancing" to Do Cultural Work in America 69
Bernice Johnson Reagon

Cultural Diversity: An Asian American Perspective 83
Margo Machida

American Indians, European Contact,
and the Doctrine of Discovery 89
Gawanahs, Tonya Gonnella Frichner

A Vision for Black Community Reconstruction 95
David Bryan

The Purposeful Underdevelopment of Latino and
Other Communities of Color 103
Marta Moreno Vega

Linking Missions and Resources
Across International Boundaries 109
Esi Sutherland-Addy

III. New Meanings

African American Cultural Empowerment: A Struggle to
Identify and Institutionalize Ourselves as a People 119
Kalamu ya Salaam

Cultural Pluralism: A Goal to Be Realized 135
Antonia Pantoja & Wilhelmina Perry

Blacks in the Diaspora:
Redefinitions for the Third Millenium 149
Rex Nettleford

Ghosts 159
Peter H. Pennekamp

From California to Nova Hispania:
Reflections on the Cultural Debates 165
Guillermo Gómez-Peña

Appendix
Cultural Diversity Based on Cultural Grounding II 177
Ratification Statement

Contributors 181

Index 187

FOREWORD

The chief problem facing the United States of America in the twenty-first century will be cultural equity. In the twentieth century, race, just as W.E.B. DuBois predicted, has been the main one. When DuBois looked at the American nation at the top of the century, he saw the lingering and continuing results of the birth of a nation in racial strife, nurtured on the unequal treatment of Africans and Europeans, and destined for conflict.

Since DuBois's 1903 insight, the United States, in its population, has come to reflect the world. No longer is that population seen in black and white, but in the technicolor of scores of cultures that have come to these shores—resulting in the enrichment of the American experience. In many ways, the U.S., not Japan, holds the key to the future of cultural interaction. While Japan has moved aggressively in the economic realm, it is still the U.S. that keeps the vision of a multicultural, multiethnic nation alive in the world. Such a vision is a predicament of the American Creed.

Of course, as the authors of this book know, the Creed and the Deed have often been completely at odds; in fact, it is difficult to say that the nation has ever lived up to the Creed. But it sounds good, because it is based on the fundamental principles of peace, equity, justice, and goodwill. Few would see those principles as being contrary to the best interests of the nation and the world. Therefore, as we seek justice and peace in the world, we begin with the condition of the United States itself. The Creed and the Deed must unite in the grand picture of a multicultural society.

It is impossible to foist onto a multicultural society a monocultural symbol system or a monocultural education system. Most human beings reject any system that dehumanizes them or trivializes their culture or their achievements. Between the real multicultural basis of this society and the attempts to maintain a monocultural education system lies a profound incongruence, in which originate the unequal positions of the many sectors of society.

What the contributors to this volume seek is that which is in the best interests of the nation and the world: a society based on cultural equity, rather than on inequality. There is ample evidence that the time for Eurocentric cultural domination is over, as it should have been long ago. In an interactive world, where peoples of every region and culture come together to create possibilities, it is not possible or right for one group to seek hegemony over another. This means that you cannot have cultural equity where European culture parades as if it is universal and all other cultures are subcultures. We are on this earthen satellite together, and we need to truly understand the meaning of cultural equity. Ours must be a movement away from the fortress mentality to the open plains of involvement and knowledge. Only then can we rise from the mediocrity fostered by inequity and reach the heights of human genius.

What this book seeks to show us is the validity, the power, and the truth of genuine human striving for cultural equity. The authors are clear about what is needed and how it should be gained. We must work toward a system of co-cultures in which equity is the primary foundation.

Molefi Kete Asante
Temple University
Philadelphia, Pennsylvania

ACKNOWLEDGMENTS

This book is a joint production that reflects the thinking and collaboration of a community of individuals too numerous to mention. It is important, however, that we acknowledge those who worked on the nuts and bolts that hold the project together and those who realize that we are in this fight for cultural equity for the long haul.

Thanks to Laura Moreno, Melody Capote, C. Daniel Dawson, Gayle Louison, Harry Newman, Pamela Francis, Mikal Muharrar, Dan'etta Adewole-Jiminez—the present and former staff of the Caribbean Cultural Center, who always make things happen. Special thanks to Dudley Cocke, Pedro Rodriguez, Antonia Pantoja, Amalia Mesa-Bains, Baraka Sele, Olga Garay, Peter Pennekamp, Tonya Gonnella Frichner, Molefi Kete Asante, Kariamu Welsh Asante, Peter Blackman, and the others who continue to establish networks and connections that clarify thought and praxis.

Thanks to Cheryll Y. Greene, my co-editor, of Cheryll Y. Greene Editorial Services for guiding the Caribbean Cultural Center's first publication into reality. And thanks to Tracie Morris of the Caribbean Cultural Center and to Gina Dorcely and Marpessa Dawn Outlaw, who assisted Cheryll Greene, for their editorial assistance on this project.

Thanks to the Rockefeller Foundation and staff: Alberta Arthurs, Susan Sato, and Tomas Ybarra Frausto for partial funding of the publication.

And of course, my very special thanks to all of the contributors to the book for their patience and dedication. The work we have embarked upon, of shifting a hegemonic paradigm to one of racial and cultural equity, may not be a reality in our lifetime, but it will be achieved for the benefit of future generations.

Marta Moreno Vega

INTRODUCTION

From its inception in 1976, the Caribbean Cultural Center has focused on uniting the many cultures of the African Diaspora with our root cultures in Africa. The shared racial and cultural histories, as well as similar contemporary experiences, provide the common ground that demands the unification of our groups. The decontextualized history of our people, the holocaust of the Middle Passage, chattel slavery, historic segregation, and miseducation, and the ongoing systemic racism and cultural inequities that persist necessitate that our histories and experiences not be told from the perspective of the hegemonic few, but from the humanistic perspective of the many who seek equity.

The work of the Caribbean Cultural Center has expanded in the last five years. We have recognized that other racial and cultural groups have suffered similar experiences of attempted genocide, political exclusion, and racial, cultural, and economic marginalization. The creation and implementation of our biannual international conferences, Cultural Diversity Based on Cultural Grounding, reflects the Center's expansion. An international advisory group composed of institution builders grounded in the cultures and needs of their communities formulates the issues, concerns, and conference topics that reflect the ongoing battles being faced by communities of color and poor white rural communities. To our knowledge, this ongoing process is the first time that cultural workers have come together from Native, Asian, African, African American, Caribbean, Latino, and Anglo communities to discuss and formulate cultural policy, actively set forth an agenda, and advance action that jointly addresses the inequities being faced by our communities and cultural organizations.

Around the world, it is now fashionable to articulate, assume, and commodify multicultural ways. The communities at issue (those of color as well as rural white communities), however, continue to receive fewer resources and lose disproportionately more institutions in periods of economic crisis. The policy decisions that create crises for culturally grounded organizations further weaken the communities that face a constant battle for survival, while the hegemonic structures that maintain Eurocentric cultural practices as the ideal are disproportionately supported. Consequently, it is the Eurocentric vision that defines, frames, and curates the works of communities of color and rural white communities. Authentic voices—grounded, validated, and trained by their communities—are most often marginalized because of inaccessibility to the recognized public forums and institutions that are designated authorities in the business of culture and arts.

Communities of color and poor rural white communities, however, are the experts in their own cultural traditions, creative expressions, and institution building processes. They insist on giving first voice to their realities, yet continue to be dismissed by Eurocentric arts and funding institutions, which impose their ethnic-specific aesthetics on a mythical global paradigm.

Voices from the Battlefront is the first of a series of publications that will voice the thinking, concerns, recommendations, and practices of people grounded in the cultures of their communities to an international public. Like all of the Caribbean Cultural Center's efforts, it reflects a collaborative, inclusive process that ensures that the product incorporates a broad input. The essays you will read in this book contain the voices of people on the front lines in the battle to ensure that our communities not only survive, but thrive in an environment of cultural equity. This book's objective is to set forth ideas, policy, and recommended practices, while advancing racial and cultural equity and desired modes of being and practice.

The larger goal is a paradigm shift from one of dominance for some to one of cultural equity for everyone. Creating this shift has been the work of the international organizing committee of the two Cultural Diversity Based on Cultural Grounding Conferences that took place in New York City in 1989 and 1991, both developed and coordinated by the Caribbean Cultural Center. The international representatives to these conferences agreed that no policy statement existed nationally or internationally that addressed the criteria and practices for establishing cultural equity internationally. Our collective work since then has focused on a multidisciplinary approach, which brings together international representatives who are cultural workers, scholars, policymakers, educators, humanists, artists, institution builders, and visionaries. The conference presenters and workshops set forth topic areas and a work plan to meet the stated objectives. Below are the major points addressed:

1. The need to establish a working lexicon that standardizes cultural terminology. The 1991 conference established a committee to develop a glossary, which will provide cultural workers with functional definitions for terms such as multiculturalism, pluralism, diversity, and so forth. *Multiculturalism* has incorrectly become the catch-all phrase for racial and cultural diversity. The fact is that multiculturalism exists within each of our racial groups. Africans, Native Americans, Asians, and Europeans have a range of cultural experiences within their racial groupings. *Pluralism*, as defined by *Webster's Ninth New Collegiate Dictionary*, is closer to the ideal concept: "a state of society in which members of diverse ethnic, racial, religious or social groups maintain an autonomous participation in and development of their traditional culture or special interest within the confines of a common civilization." (Although preferable to *multiculturalism*, the phrase "common civilization" contained in the dictionary's definition is also problematic because most of our racial and cultural groups have been similarly oppressed by hegemonic groups that forced "common civilization" upon varied communities.) *Diversity* recognizes distinct elements or qualities, yet fails, as do the other terms, to address issues of racial, cultural and economic *equity*. We seek parity, and the language we use must reflect and define this idea.

2. The need to establish a common language grounded in the principles of equity and parity, which is critical to establishing a

paradigm that recognizes the diverse aesthetic criteria for excellence.

This book is a primer, a hands-on tool for those like us engaged in the fight for racial and cultural equity. The struggle for us alone has been one that spans 500 years in the Americas. Despite the barriers we face, our communities continue to envision a future where equality is grounded in humanistic traditional values that respect spiritual and natural forces. If we are to be successful in our quest, it is imperative that we learn from each other, respect our differences, and recognize our common ground. The contributors to this publication reflect the racial and cultural diversity that is grounded in their unique experiences.

The process of getting to know one another, agreeing, and even disagreeing, forges the working relationships needed among people in communities worldwide. As this book goes to print, regional conferences on cultural equity are being held in the United States and England. It is through this ongoing sharing and meeting of equals that change must occur. Each of us is part of this important process. Our commitment and will to generate change will make it happen. *Voices from the Battlefront* reflects the thinking of representatives nurtured by their communities on the front lines of the struggle to shift the paradigm of dominance to one of equity. It comes from contributors dedicated to transformation and liberation for us all. I urge you to seek out and participate in their work and their organizations. Their voices are the voices of our communities, speaking directly to you.

Marta Moreno Vega

PART I
FRAMEWORKS

RETHINKING WHO WE ARE

A BASIC DISCUSSION
OF BASIC TERMS

John Kuo Wei Tchen

The words of Trinh Minh-ha, a filmmaker and a philosopher, kept coming back to me as I was preparing for these remarks. She talks about the importance of what she calls the "interval." In the case of the term *Asian American*, for example, the interval is that space between the two contrasting cultural constructs that designates a third, often yet to be realized, place that transcends the attributed polar exclusivity of being Asian and of being American. In Daoist imagination, the seeds of change and transformation are always within what appears to be the status quo. In critiquing the way things are, we also gain the beginnings of alternative visions of the future. This conference, then, offers an important nuturing place in which we can reflect upon praxis past and rededicate ourselves for future battles. It is in this spirit that I offer these remarks.

I'd like to make a few comments on some underlying ideas that are so pervasive in United States life that, like the air we breathe, they are invisible, yet omnipresent. These popular and powerful ideas are so much a part of the basic ways in which we

This essay is based on a presentation given at the Cultural Diversity Based on Cultural Grounding II Conference in New York City, October 17-18, 1991. Tchen was part of a panel that addressed the issue "Cultural Paradigm for Equity: Defining the Philosophical Framework and Steps of Implementation."

think of ourselves and others that we seldom consider what they are truly about. The simple declarative statement "We are modern individuals living in a pluralistic, democratic society" embodies much of what Americans would say about themselves. Now, let's dissect the phrase and analyze the ideological baggage it contains.

First of all, *we* is a nationalist term still used in this increasingly global, trans- and international world. Despite this culture's fascination with encounters of the third kind, it resolutely stands for those who are inaccurately self-designated as *Americans*—which only truly means those of the United States. Of course, we can immediately sense some of the limits and complications of such binary terms. Does *we* necessarily mean a legal citizen? What if due to racist laws a person of color is not allowed to become a citizen? Why are Asians who have been in this country for generations still viewed as foreigners by virtue of their "look"?

In addition, *we* is juxtaposed to *them,* which presumably refers to peoples of other nations and cultures who do not necessarily have this combination of qualities we believe we embody. We are modern. We are individuals. We are pluralistic. And, we are democratic. They, this line of thinking goes, probably are not.

Let's examine this proposition in terms of being a *modern* people. Being modern in United States consumer-based culture has largely meant a radical fragmentation of time. Modernity is separated from "tradition," and the past has been forever relegated to the "dustbin" of how this society thinks of "history." This splitting of past from future strikes violently at the heart of many "old-" and "new-" world cultures from which most of us come. The insistence on that separation constantly befuddles many new immigrants, still steeped in other ways of being, and it constantly discourages all Americans from grounding themselves in their own personal and social genealogies. If we choose to define ourselves as modern and progressive peoples, we necessarily think of ourselves as nontraditional. Who wants to be thought of as "backward"?! A conceit of modernity is that it is rational and objective. Ghosts, for example, don't live in the modern world.

Fei Xiaotung, the preeminent Chinese sociologist who studied in the United States in the 1930s, once reflected on what he felt to be most lacking in American society. Americans' optimistic faith in ever-brighter technological progress, he felt, betrayed a serious weakness—that being a lack of any belief in ghosts. Mind you, this was a sophisticated man who was ultimately commenting on what he perceived to be the fervent and unhealthy American penchant for separating the present from the past, and the past from the future. Americans, Dr. Fei believed, had blinders on. They tended not to learn from the past, nor did they think about the well-being of future generations. From a contemporary ecological perspective alone, we can agree with his point. Certainly all those return-of-the-living-dead movies of Grandma and Uncle Bill invading suburbia to eat their irreverent offspring betray some very real social tensions. Americans are constantly running away from what is "old" and running toward some unknown "newness," always defined as "better."

There's a terrific quote that explores a transcendant synthesis of this otherwise no-win, dead-end way of life, in Albert Murray's *The Hero and the Blues*. I'd like to share it with you.

Essentially, questions about experimentation and the arts are also questions about the relevance of tradition. They're questions about the practical application of traditional elements to contemporary problem situations. Hence, they are also questions about change and continuity. Indeed, they are specifically concerned with the requirements for continuation, which is to say, endurance, which is also to say, survival. Implicitly, experimentation is also an action taken to ensure that nothing endures which is not workable. As such, far from being anti-traditional, as is often assumed, it actually serves the best interests of tradition.

We have to resist the simple-minded conceits of being "modern," for that is one of the ways in which we disempower ourselves.

Another loaded term is the word *individual*. Now, of course, we are all biological individuals separate from one another physiologically and existentially. Fine, but does that mean we all believe in the ideology of individualism above all other social relations? Or does being an individualist necessarily mean one is not a part of a group identity? American films, my Rorschach test for those invisible air-like values that bind our common culture together, certainly testify to the pervasive separation of individual from group. The classic American hero, from Rocky to Thelma and Louise to that cute, obnoxious kid in *Home Alone*, is one who stands outside of the family and the crowd to realize their true inner selves.

Can't we believe in individual freedom and also believe in being group members? Well, yes (we are told), but only as part of a subcultural (and therefore exotic and somewhat strange) expression—not as part of the mainstream tradition. European Enlightenment *philosophes* have emphasized individual, white, male freedom and rationality. And political economists have trumpeted economic or possessive individualism. The logic of *the more we consume, the more we waste, the more we throw away, the better we are able to find, express, and define ourselves* may be great for the Gross National Product, but is otherwise disastrous. Many of us come from traditional cultures in which, if we eat animal flesh, it is with the ethic of eating or using all parts of the animal, paying respects to the sources of the food and clothing, and trying to be frugal so there will be enough to go around. These seemingly "old-fashioned" ideas clearly need to be a part of this nation's outlook for the near future, lest we consume the entire globe.

The next key term in my simple sentence is *pluralism*. This term is used loosely and as an unquestioned good. Certainly, we want this nation to think and be more diverse than it has ever been, but is this notion already embodied in the idea of pluralism? The term itself has a history that needs serious exploration, but let me focus on its most common popular meanings and uses. It is often used as a shorthand way to celebrate, often uncritically, the diversity of this nation's peoples. The mythic symbolism of Puritans and Native Americans sitting down over cranberries and turkey, Emma Lazarus's version of what the Statue of Liberty is about, and the "encounter" of the "old" world's cultures in this supposed "new" world all signal a sort of sacred reverence and patriotism for who we are. Americans from all the world's cultures sitting down to a common Yankee meal was an image that political cartoonist Thomas Nast expressed in the 1870s, and it is still expressed today.

Now, given the rules of American modernity and possessive

individualism, we can best achieve the promise of pluralistic inclusion only if we become "Americanized" and heartily subscribe to a sort of blind faith. In addition, inclusion is premised on an expanding economic pie. The pie distributor tells us: Be patient, be good, and someday soon you too will benefit. Those of us involved in day-to-day struggles of surviving and working in the 1990s know that the pie has not been getting any bigger lately. In fact, it has been made to appear smaller and smaller. For the moment, never mind that from 1977 to 1987 the top 1 percent of the U.S. population had doubled its wealth, thereby owning more than all of the bottom 90 percent. Whatever the reason for the shrinking pie, we need to understand that pluralism, or this ideology of inclusiveness, has always been premised on the pie getting bigger. In an essentially zero-growth economy that is simultaneously becoming more diverse and more unequal, doesn't the rhetoric of pluralism get stretched precariously thin?

Finally, the term *democracy* needs some scrutiny. Clearly the term can take on lots of different meanings in different contexts and to different peoples. But it has mainly been defined in terms of the electoral act of voting for political "leaders" who will largely make top-down decisions critical to our lives and the lives of future generations. Of course, we also have opinion polls, which purportedly express the voice of the people. Presidential candidate Ross Perot's ideal of American democracy is an "electronic town hall" in which citizens call 900 numbers to be automatically tabulated as a "supporter" of his campaign. Clearly, such technologically defined gimmicks of participatory democracy are anemic at best and antidemocratic at worst. The older, time-tested means of generating grassroots and group consensus are dismissed as too inefficient and prone to demagogic manipulation. Yet our "modern," "individualistic," and "pluralist" culture seems to progressively devalue genuine dialogue, consensus building, and grassroots participation. The old town square, once the place for public discourse, has been abandoned, with the rest of our inner cities, in favor of shiny, privatized palaces of mass consumption—you know, shopping malls.

Instead, I prefer drawing on a diversity of our older traditions that can reinvigorate the meaning of democracy. Now our political culture tells us that Asian societies tend to be "despotic" and don't practice true "democracy," in the electoral sense. Even if this were true, Americans tend to assume Asian cultures have been strictly and essentially totalitarian nightmares. How then can we explain the various humanist social philosophies of Asia that prized social caring and responsiblity and were grounded in the relation of the natural and human worlds? How can we explain away the thoughts of someone like Zhuangtzu (Chuang Tze), the third century B.C. Daoist philosopher who advocated popular dialogue and critical thinking skills. He stated:

> A basket trap is for catching fish, but when one has got the fish, one need not think any more about the basket. A foot trap is for catching hares, but when one has got the hare, one need think no more about the trap. Words are for holding ideas, but when one has got the idea, one need no longer think about the words. If only I could find someone who had stopped thinking about words and could have him with me to talk to.

This suggestive quote is part of a long tradition of popular philosophy that in this country has been reduced to Charlie Chan and fortune cookie aphorisms. A statement like Zhuangtzu's was not meant to tell you what to think, but to evoke thoughts and discussion. A view such as this not only underscores the importance of the process of genuine dialogue, as opposed to the rhetorical fetish about celebrating electoral democracy, but it also, in a rather unexpected and basic way, explores the prerequisites necessary for engaging in dialogue. One must first have the tools for survival and communication (a basket trap and literacy) in order to be able to engage in a fair discussion. Is this understood in the American practice of democracy? Except for the periodic emergence of radical democratic movements in this nation's history, our form of electoral democracy tends to slumber when it comes to making it mean more than the occasional act of voting.

Let me reiterate the ideological sentence that inhabits the air we breathe: "We are modern individuals living in a pluralistic, democratic society." I hope that after this basic dissection of these basic terms, such a sentence is far more problematic than it has ever appeared. We need to critique the way these words are normally thought of, reinvigorate and redefine the words themselves so they take on better and braver meanings, and perhaps invent new words with even more resonant and inclusive definitions. And, as many people attending this conference already know, we need to rededicate ourselves to reconstructing American society. Social movements pushing for expansion of human rights have always been a motive and progressive force in this nation's history. To truly make these and other words sing to our hearts, we have to build popular, grassroots places for engaged and meaningful dialogue about who we are becoming.

AFROCENTRICITY

A PHILOSOPHICAL BASIS
FOR CULTURAL EQUITY BATTLES?

Harold Cruse

It is with great pleasure that I am able to speak with you this afternoon, for the simple reason that at this particular time in our history many of the issues that are prominent on your agenda are issues with which I have been grappling for the last twenty-five years. As a matter of fact, my whole writing career, you might say, has been involved and concerned with many of the ideas that have been expressed here—except that, I must confess, the range and scope of the topics discussed here represent a rather grand enlargement on my original ideas on the general topic. Right now, however, I'm going to be only exploratory. But I'd like to throw out to you some critical questions about the general topic of this session, "Cultural Paradigm for Equity: Defining the Philisophical Framework and Steps of Implementation," with the goal of perhaps enlarging on the scope of the paradigm that we are discussing now.

First of all, it is very significant that a discussion of this kind is taking place in the United States, the historical, economic, military, cultural, and philosophical pinnacle of Western civilization at this stage. More than that, this conference takes place in New York City, the capital of that same grand pinnacle of the West. And here we are, talking about a restructuring of the cultural and philo-

---

This presentation was the keynote address of the panel "Cultural Paradigm for Equity: Defining the Philosophical Framework and Steps of Implementation" at the Cultural Diversity Based on Cultural Grounding II Conference in New York City on October 17, 1991.

sophical scope of the African Diaspora and about its impact on a New World. Here, the term *New World* is used to describe the concept as it was popularized following Christopher Columbus's "discovery." This so-called New World became the geographical land mass for the transportation, settlement, and expansion of multiple branches and components of the African Diaspora. We're trying to define the impact this Diaspora is going to have on the twenty-first century. We are saying, in effect, that now is the time to start examining this very important question. As we all know, that's a pretty big order—as is projecting notions of a cultural paradigm for equity. But, as we're saying, now is the time.

AFROCENTRICITY: A NEW PHILOSOPHICAL FRAMEWORK

First of all, we have to be fully aware, or fully cognizant, of all the ingredients that have gone into the movement since the 1960s, leading to this moment. And we must take all of these differences, these movements, these expressions, these phases into consideration in order to create even the semblance of a new cultural paradigm for equity—new definitions that will include a number of philosophical refinements of our view of this process leading from the Civil Rights Movement of the 1960s to the present. On the philosophical level what has occurred is that many of the ideological components of the last thirty years have now been put into a new intellectual framework, which is called Afrocentricity. In other words, the philosophical content of the new paradigm, for many, has already been established. This means, first off, that Afrocentricity itself has to be looked at from a very critical standpoint, in terms of its diasporic validity. Its validity has to be based on the historical experiences and phases of development of the Diaspora in the United States and the rest of the New World, the impact of Western civilization on the thinking of the diasporic components —all of this toward a new world order, a new world order within the Diaspora itself, a new framework, because, as has been said, our present framework is insufficient. If that is the case, the question is *why?*

We know the framework of the Civil Rights Movement of the last thirty years. The movement was social and political, ideological, and so forth. The problem with it, despite our emphasis now on the cultural side of the question, is that the movement itself was not specifically cultural in its projections. The cultural aspects were only vestigial, that is to say, the movement resulted in a belated outpouring of various cultural and artistic manifestations on the part of the American Black population. These cultural expressions had a history, of course, going back to the nineteenth, eighteenth, and seventeenth centuries. The Civil Rights aims, generally speaking, led in an integrationist direction that had nothing at all to do with the creation of a type of cultural organization such as the Caribbean Cultural Center. Such a group was only hinted at then. This integrationist focus becomes problematic if we are to talk about developing an Afrocentric philosophical model.

Such a model, unlike that posited during the early days of the Civil Rights Movement in the sixties, takes us back, reorients us to the beginnings, you can say, of the African experience prior to our New World experience in the United States. And it raises the question of how we conceptually combine the two prevailing concepts of culture—the artistic and the anthropological—into a working philosophical format that addresses our position in the United States and within the Diaspora. It says that we have to bring all of these ingredients—historical, social, political, cultural—within the context of a new dynamic, a new paradigm, in order to deal both contemporaneously and historically with our position here today. That is a mighty big order. And we better get it right now, we better work this thing out right, make it philosophically effective, work it out so that it impacts on our situation in the New World today. It's got to impact on our situation *today*, not just be concerned with the beginnings of civilization in Egypt, or with the best of Africa, but it must affect us *today*. It's got to work out that way. Or else it remains an abstraction. A philosophical abstraction. And this we must keep in mind.

No one individual is going to reach this goal alone, by the way. I'm not going to do it alone. The people at Temple University, who originated the Afrocentricity concept, are not going to do it alone, either. It's going to take the thinking of our best minds to reconstruct the diasporic experience in Afrocentric terms as an approach to twenty-first century existence. That's a big order. Nevertheless, we've seen its beginnings. Now, this does not call, in my view, for an endless discussion of the impact or the meaning of Black ancient classicism. We can discuss that; it's a very important historical issue. We need the discussion for our own self-education, we need to go back and look at these ancient problems, ancient philosophies, ancient religions. I would contend that the arguments that probably went on in Ancient Egypt are the same arguments going on right here in New York today, on the questions of *who is who? who was who?* and *who is the most important who?* So, our aim is nothing new. It's ancient; it's a current concern, and it's going round to the twenty-first century, the same argument about the origin of civilization.

But what is more important for us today is how we assess what is the totality, the contemporary end product of Western hemispheric civilization, containing as it does the various branches and components of the African Diaspora, and how this diasporic outcome will become more and more problematic from now into the twenty-first century. No matter what intellectual approach we use to formulate our conclusions on this matter, we face a formidable intellectual task. So, given the challenges, there is much material that we have to reinvestigate if we are going to talk about Afrocentricity and its outcome in terms of cultural or political discourse for the next century—because the problem of the absence of cultural equity is going to remain.

RESPONSIBILITIES AND CHALLENGES

As approaches to our situation, I have never seriously argued against integrationism, as such, or argued for separation as such. These are parts of the baggage coming out of nineteenth-century Black thinking—separatism, integrationism, assimilationism, back-to-Africa-ism, and so forth. The problem here is how to integrate these ingredients into a working cultural philosophy that can attack the question of lack of equity at this stage of the game. The political—the Black Power—phase of the 1960s Civil Rights Movement, the gestures toward group consolidation for political empowerment within Black communities, was misused and squandered after a certain amount of political know-how was developed and recognition achieved. No organizational forms followed that

phase of the movement, no palpable representations of any organizational expressions of Black Power. How can political power or
cultural power be established without organization?

What it means, then, as we go into the twenty-first century,
is that we are grappling with the problem of resources, and we
don't have many. Where will the resources come from to carry on
the work of this organization or others around the country toward
the goal of cultural equity?

Cultural equity is not going to be achieved by talk and grand
declarations about our ambitions on this score. It's not going to be
accomplished that way. It's only going to happen if, as a consequence of this sort of conference, for example, those involved can
redirect their organizational approaches to the African American
class stratifications with which we will have to deal in our
Afrocentric projects for the twenty-first century.

One of the stratifications we have to deal with, aside from the
cultural personalities themselves, is the new Black middle class.
Most of our outstanding cultural personalities are in this new class.
We have been imbued with the notion that we have to glorify cultural heroes, whoever they are, whatever they're doing. The sweet
smell of success, you see, is what we glamorize. That's all right—
I've got no real argument with that, particularly as the Civil Rights
Movement developed. It's what the movement asked for, isn't it?
For the right to be "successful," to achieve, to be recognized, and to
garner all the rewards thereby from this great, rich society. This
has been uppermost in the minds of most all American Blacks from
the very beginning: achievement and equity—political, economic,
educational equity, and so forth, but based on the conceptual
premise of racial integration, that is, on the individual basis.

This becomes problematic—and it applies not only to our cultural activists, our cultural icons, it also involves our intellectuals, our professionals, all of our institutions, particularly colleges,
civil rights organizations, all of the institutions and organizational forms that represent the full scope of Black people's existence
in the United States. These have to come under a new examination. Unless this is done, there isn't going to be any change in our
priorities going into the twenty-first century.

I want to suggest this much, this scheme. I believe that from now to the year 2000 our Black elites in this country have got to be reeducated about their responsibilities to the group experience in this country. They've had their spree, they've had their fun, they've had their achievement, they've been on TV—too much, in fact. They've been sent around the world as ambassadors of the Black experience in the United States, and so on. They've been to Africa, two or three times. Everyone's accepted them as celebrities. They've had their day. But what are their cultural responsibilities? Where lie the responsibilities of top sports figures and others to the political and socioeconomic advances of their own group, to their own people down below who heroize them, who honor them? They don't contribute very much to these people. They leave that to the federal government.

Now here comes the challenge—for the Caribbean Cultural Center conference and all of us involved here. Looking at it another way, it's a problem of leadership. That's the big issue.

A problem of leadership and the lack of it. There is no leadership out there, up there, you see, that the people down there look up to. None of those up there are telling themselves what they are supposed to be doing, organizationally, institutionally, financially, economically. The Black colleges, professional organizations, sports figures—all of them have got to be told that we, as a group, must learn how to function the way other racial and ethnic groups function in this society. They function through cooperative endeavor, cooperative economic endeavor. Those who have access to funds contribute funds—that's what they do.

Now, this has been said for generations among Blacks themselves: We do not cooperate economically, that is why we get nowhere. But a historical question is also opened up by this critique of the elites today, what their function is or ought to be, and what they represent or don't represent—because it's not a new question, it's an old question.

LINKAGES TO AFRICA

Another crucial matter: Afrocentricity, as our new philosophical style of thinking, in many ways sums up on an intellectual level what we have been trying to express ever since before Emancipation. How do we establish links to the African continent?

This matter of linkages has been talked about for over 100 years, and nothing substantial has been done about it organizationally or institutionally. Don't think this is not our responsibility today, that we're not called upon to look back and retrace this issue of our linkages with the African continent and how we have handled the matter historically. I'll tell you what: We have messed it up. Or it has been messed up for us. And I'll tell you something else: The biggest mess-up was Marcus Garvey. After all that effort, he left no institution behind. A tradition must be built on what a leader accomplishes and what he or she leaves behind to be picked up on, carried on over the next hundred years.

So, the glorification of these Back-to-Africa movements has been overdrawn, uncritically heroized. By approaching the subject this way, we are neglecting to understand where the movements and leaders failed, why they failed, and what the consequences are for today. We can't afford that any more if we are talking about Afrocentricity—which requires a revival and reexamination of the ideas and contentions and intentions of these movements. And an understanding of why we are left having to pick up the reins at this late date. Unless we take these steps—from a philosophical, intellectual, and organizational point of view—Afrocentricity will not meet its goal of establishing a new critique in these matters.

I'll end with this idea: With regard to the African continent, the Diaspora, and all the factors that we have discussed, the big question on the international political agenda right now is the South African question. That's the biggest item on the agenda, even in terms of Afrocentricity. That question is going to have to be ultimately resolved with the complicity of Blacks in the United States. And we better get ready for it. History seems to indicate that in the long overview of the Diaspora, the connection of the people in this hemisphere with the African continent rests on the very latest of the emergency conditions on that continent—and that unless we are involved in the settlement of whatever that issue is, it's not going to be settled in the interests of Africans themselves over there. I don't think we see that. And we're not prepared for it. In the same way that we haven't been prepared organizationally or economically, and so on, to maintain ongoing organizational ties with the African continent, in that same way we're not prepared today to be involved in the resolution of the South African question.

I'll end there.

Ed. note: An extended and lively question-and-answer session followed Dr. Cruse's presentation. Here are a few key excerpts.

Q: I'd like to ask Harold Cruse to identify the ten most important issues that Black intellectuals must resolve in order for us to move, in the twenty-first century, to a culturally, economically, and politically viable position.

A: Well, I think there are more than ten issues, but that's a good beginning. Now, as I said in my earlier remarks, the area that I was scheduled to cover is a large one, and each issue is worth extended discussions. In other words, this session itself has been basically exploratory; it has extended the horizons of our thinking. So, I'm challenged in attempting to answer all this in a discrete way.

The question is the ten most important issues that intellectuals must face for the next century. One is the necessity of extending the conceptual range of operations of an organization like the Caribbean Cultural Center. Two, I would say, as I intimated in talking about the Black Power phase, is how to overcome the limitations of our two-party political system, which governs our political thinking—how to overcome and break up the two-party grip, not only on minorities, as it were, but on the whole nation. It's a national problem here, and it's my long-standing belief that people of color have the only potential of acting politically in the interests of the entire nation. That's how I see particularly the Black presence in the United States. I've always thought this. Our movements have been necessarily limited in scope, because they were aimed at the achievement of immediate goals, not distant goals. A lot of the immediate goals have been achieved, after a fashion.

Number three, the intellectuals among us have got to give new organizational meaning to the African connection with the Diaspora. Declarations and idealistic expressions are not going to achieve what we are talking about. The connection has got to be put into organizational form if it's going to have any impact at all, whether international or domestic, particularly with regards to people in our communities. Those who are lower down the economic level are informed about international conditions through television, for the most part. But there is no middle-level leadership that's in a position to explain exactly what is going on. Without these achievements by intellectuals, I don't see us in the twenty-first century accruing anything substantial in the international arena, considering the distribution of power that exists today. This is a very real issue. How can we overcome this organizationally? We have the numbers. We have the resources in terms of people, but we don't have the levers to accomplish this.

On the cultural front, Americans don't view Black intellectuals or any other group as having the intellectual wherewithal to have an impact on world philosophy. They don't believe that anyone can create new philosophies at this late stage. They believe that the philosophical tradition coming out of Greece and the Western tradition has said it all. So it's a formidable intellectual challenge, but if Black intellectuals are going to make any impact internationally during the twenty-first century, we have got to reconstruct a philosophical outlook on life and attempt to codify it. The philosophy of Afrocentricity must be codified—in the same way that European philosophies codified their conclusions and their assumptions for people to look at and read about.

I would like to believe that in the new era people of African descent in the New World–Western Hemisphere will ultimately have as much impact on which way the world turns as the Western philosophers had in previous centuries. I think it's possible, but it's going to require a lot of effort, a lot of conferences, debates, and problem-solving going into the next century. More important, it's going to require organization, organizational forms coming into existence through which to express new conclusions about the relationship between East and West, North and South, hemispheric relations among all the peoples of color that have been talked about here today. Or else, we are going to lapse into a long, drawn-out period, similar to what we've been told existed during the Middle Ages. A new Dark Age is going to settle on this hemisphere, on this globe, unless people of color, particularly those in the Western Hemisphere, take matters into their own hands.

What are the other issues? They are subsumed under point three, as far as I'm concerned.

Q: Dr. Cruse, could you discuss which institutions, in your opinion, have existed that would be models or guides as we have forged community institutions over the past twenty years, such as the Caribbean Cultural Center, which is now sixteen years old? Or the DuBois Center in Ghana, or the National Black Arts Festival, which is developing in Atlanta? There are a number of institutions that came out of the sixties struggles that have been attempting to address the kinds of issues you bring up, and over the past two days here, an internal dialogue has been going on among representatives of developing institutions.

A: The first step would be, in my view, to bring these various groups into some form of coalition, some form of leadership coalition. Once you achieve that, I would suggest that the coalition take on a national aspect. Then they should sit down in a conference like this one and work out regional strategies to deal with the national issues. Then, as a nationally oriented group, begin to speak to the various Black elites around the country with the message of what we expect them to be involved in. As we've discussed, the issue is a national one—and also an international one.

As we've also pointed out, generally the elites don't think this way. They're provincial, in that they believe their own existence, achievements, and visibility are the most important things. But don't blame the situation on them entirely. Blame it on our lack of leadership expression, which results in a failure to inform these people how they should be functioning, how they should be thinking. If nobody informs them or "tells them off," there's going to be a long period ahead of trying to convince them of what their social, political, and cultural obligations are. I'm confident that the atmosphere, the condition in this country is going to be such that the elites are going to be forced to respond. Because their future's up for grabs, too. They might think they're safely ensconced now as elites in their work, their professions, or whatever. But their future is not assured. The eighties showed us this, if nothing else. The only way to assure their future is through some organizational expression of their own that can give direction to the larger society.

Let's face it: We have developed an elite class that falls into the category of being a clientage group. Their status is predicated on what the establishment up there gives them, what the government and the corporations give them. They are members of a powerless clientage group that possesses no internal power of its own to determine the policies of this society. That's what it amounts to. And they've got to be made aware of this—of what they really are, not what they imagine themselves to be. They didn't make it into the elite on their own, as some of them claim. Some did on an individual basis, but in general the stage was actually set by the top-level elites in this country and by the government elites. They created the conditions for the existence of this new clientage group of Black elites, who are dependent on them. And these Blacks are selected on that premise. When President Bush selected Clarence Thomas, for example, he selected him as a client, and Thomas or others in that position become important only because they have been picked for this role.

SETTING THE RECORD STRAIGHT

A VIEW FROM SENECA COUNTRY

G. Peter Jemison

At the present time I live on the site of a seventeenth-century Seneca town, a Seneca town that was destroyed by a campaign of the French in 1687, a Seneca town known as Ganondagan that became a national historic landmark in 1964, a Seneca town that became a New York State historic site in 1987. Among the thirty-five sites that the New York State Office of Parks, Recreation and Historic Preservation maintains, it is the only one dedicated to a Native American theme. To give you some sense of where we are right now, there are no historic sites in New York State under this system that are dedicated to the experiences of African Americans or Hispanic Americans or Asian Americans, or workers, or, for that matter, women. This Ganondagan is one of only a thousand national historic landmarks in the United States. There is currently an effort underway to create some additional landmarks, and I would suggest that you might want to become a part of that process, to learn how that works.

Our movement seeks the recognition of Native American artists, writers, and musicians. It relies on a conceptual reawakening of our way of life. Actually this way has never vanished, but

These remarks are based on a presentation that was part of a panel discussion, "From the Dominance of the Few to the Liberation of the Many: New Definitions," at the Cultural Diversity Based on Cultural Grounding II Conference in New York City on October 17, 1991.

most Americans still know very little about Native Americans. Our art is the indigenous art of this country, in fact. The Amercan Indian way of life goes on despite systematic attempts by the United States government to extinguish our languages and traditional ways. The government has done this by tearing children away from their families, placing them in schools, and punishing them severely for speaking their languages. Christian churches divided up Indian territory and made converts, further fragmenting our way of life. The survival of the Indian way of life that is indigenous to this country provides the framework by which all others who come to this land understand their own unique identity.

The 1990 census announces that there are 62,000 Native Amricans living in New York State. Let's compare that with the 21 million indigenous voices that were to be heard north of Mexico when the Europeans encountered Turtle Island. Many Native American nations no longer exist; they were silenced through disease and warfare, and the land was taken from them. Four hundred treaties were signed, and each one has been broken by the United States government. These are the facts; some people know them, but they are not clearly understood.

Subliminally, thinking people have understood that the land was occupied by human beings and that they did not vanish. But what happened? The story told by the textbook writers has been carefully edited for the young minds that the system wanted to mold. But we are challenging the American educational system, which has permitted amnesia to replace a truthful history. The continuing activities of our movement are forcing the system to reexamine the presentation of historical contributions of all peoples to the fabric of America. The Board of Regents for the State of New York, under the leadership of Thomas Sobel, with its report, *One Nation, Many Peoples: A Declaration of Cultural Independence*, seems to open a door. The report states: "There needs to be a significant expansion of in-service education for teachers. Multicultural education is often viewed as divisive and even as destructive to the values which hold us together as Americans. But national unity does not require that we eliminate the very diversity that is the source of our uniqueness. If the U.S. is to continue to prosper in the twenty-first century, then all of its citizens, whatever their race or ethnicity, must believe that they and their ancestors have shared in the building of the country and have a stake in its success."

I place a great emphasis on education and the future. Education for all, at all levels, including the sports fans who do the "tomahawk chop" while they're watching the Atlanta Braves, including those Senators who attend the Washington Redskins games. All must reach a point when they give up these racist attitudes toward the original people of this country. We must continue to learn from one another. The Caribbean, for example, remains a mystery for me even today. In Minneapolis recently I saw an exhibition on the Caribbean, and I realized the complexity of that region and its relationship to all the different peoples who had shaped it. And I'm sure that many of you know very little of the world I am a part of. So, I've always believed that a visual reference is the best way to talk about who we are.

This is a facsimile of a wampum belt. Wampum is not money. Wampum is actually made of the quahog clam shell. We didn't have clam shells in the inland parts of this country. The people who made this belt, of these shells and beads, were the coastal Indians, the people who resided where the Shinnecock on Long Island live today and who were the ancestors of those people. The people who lived in New England along the Atlantic coast made this wampum and traded it inland for things that they needed. This particular belt is called "The Invitation to Enter the Confederacy" belt. It depicts the five original nations that make up our Haudenosaunee Confederacy: the Seneca, the Cayuga, the Onondaga, the Oneida, and the Mohawk Nations. Later, in the 1700s, we were joined by the Tuscarora Nation, the sixth to join. We were united in our Confederacy by a man we call the Peacemaker, who journeyed among our people sometime after 900 A.D. At the creation of our Confederacy about a thousand years ago, the original belt was made—and it still exists and is held by the Onondaga Nation.

When the Peacemaker came to us, he recognized that our five nations were not the only ones who would be interested in peace or in that message of unity, or in the concept of replacing killing with thinking. And so he left behind a symbol for us: a white pine tree. We Haudenosaunee don't have a flag. We have, instead, a tree. If you ever look at the needles of the white pine tree, they grow in clusters of five, just like our original five nations. A cavity was dug at the base of the tree, and there they cast the weapons of war. And the Peacemaker said that these roots at the base of this tree will run North, South, East and West, in the four directions, and that any other people who wanted to embrace this message of peace could follow these roots back to the base of the tree and join with us. And so he left these four white roots as a route for people to come into this concept of peace, unity, justice, and the dignity of the individual.

All of these concepts are the Indian roots of American democracy. This wampum belt is a copy of the Constitution before the Europeans arrived, this wampum belt is what Benjamin Franklin was influenced by, Samuel Rutledge, James Madison, and so on. We were sitting with them in Philadelphia when they were writing the Constitution. We were answering their questions about how this sounds, does this work? But very strong counterforces were at work, very strong counterforces lobbied for the retention of slavery, could not give up that idea as a system of making money. And so centuries passed before African Americans obtained the rights that all human beings seek.

The system of democracy by which Haudenosaunee people live promised the founders of America a different type of government. It was a concept that opened the door to the system under which you live today. Our traditional system of governance consists of a Council of Chiefs, with a Grand Council that represents our Six Nations. Within the Grand Council each chief is a representative of his Nation. The Grand Council is made up of the Elder Brothers—the Seneca, the Onondaga, and the Mohawk—and the younger Brothers—the Cayuga, Oneida, and Tuscarora. The head of our Grand Council today is Todadaho, who is an Onondaga, and it is within their territory that our Grand Council convenes. We may liken the Elder Brothers to the Senate, and the Younger Brothers to the House of Representatives. Todadaho, similarly, is the equivalent of the executive branch of American government when the Grand Council is in session.

In the nineteenth century the United States imposed upon some of our people an elective system of government that they could closely monitor. Political divisions resulted, eroding the unity of our Confederacy. The U.S. Congress has assumed plenary power over Native Americans, and the American judicial system has largely failed to uphold our rights as sovereign nations. Only by American Indians insisting on our treaty rights and standing up for our sovereignty will we survive into the future.

In July 1991 the Bush administration issued its first Indian policy statement. The most recent previous one was issued by President Reagan in 1983. It remains to be seen what the end-of-century policies may turn out to be. Bush's policy affirmed self-determination and self-government for the 514 Native American nations in the U.S.—and that is to say that there are 514 governments that maintain the sovereignty of our Native people. In the language of the judiciary, Bush described these entities, our Native governments, as quasisovereign, domestic, dependent nations. His policy proposed to abolish excessive federal dependency—in other words, subtract the money. Finally, he suggested that the trust that Congress has for protecting our resources will be better managed in the future. The Department of the Interior, which is charged with this responsibility, has allowed the Bureau of Indian Affairs to be mismanaged, resulting in the loss of millions of dollars owed to American Indians for lands leased and resources such as coal mined on Indian lands. In other words, they're going to stop stealing, or helping people to steal what's ours—I'm waiting for that to happen. Our treaties were made as one nation to another nation. We have sovereignty: This has been acknowledged through the treaties, which are international law. The United States must live up to the obligations they took on when they made the treaties.

For example, when the federal government withdraws its responsibilities from Native Americans, the end result is that the state governments step in. The New York State Department of Taxation and Finance set up roadblocks recently off the Cattaraugus Reservation at Irving, New York (which, incidentally, is my original home), in order to notify truckers about tax laws regarding highway use, gasoline, and cigarettes. Truckers coming off the reservation, after having bought tax-free gas and cigarettes, were told that they have an obligation to pay taxes to New York State. They were warned that, while they weren't going to collect taxes from them then, they might do so in the future, as well as check their manifests and logs. So, the state, in other words, is prepared to erode whatever sovereignty we have at this present time.

The politics of our two societies exist and continue to evolve as the world about us changes. These changes are reflected in the work of those artists who listen to their consciences and respond to them in their art. I'm a visual artist. At the moment, my work is included in about six different exhibitions. I mention this not to brag about it, but to say that it shows how we're being given a sort of moment in the sunshine again—and we're asking ourselves whether this is the apex of the fifteen-year cycle when Indians suddenly come up again as interesting. How can we sustain access to the media—for television, newspapers, and films form or confirm people's attitudes about Indians. We must continue to correct the portrayal of Indians through the images that reach the airwaves. I suggest to you that we will be the ones to make that happen.

You and I here in this room, we are the influencers of change, we have brought it about, we wouldn't be here if we weren't capable of bringing about change. But we must also make sure that change is sustained. And so, while the outlook is bleak, while we see funding evaporating, I believe that only internal community initiative will sustain us through these next years. This is a test from the Establishment: Can you take it when I put your arm way up behind your back and squeeze real hard? You better be able to. We better all be able to.

One last word. In the early 1970s, we saw a renewed interest among Native American people in their life ways and in their cultural traditions. We, who were the young activists at that time, who were influenced by those movements, such as the American Indian Movement, and by events like The Longest Walk, are now the ones who are in the leadership positions. We're the ones who are now on the inside working for our people to see change come about. We're the ones who have obtained the law degrees, who are working for the preservation and repatriation of our sacred items, who are protecting our ancestors' remains, who are working for the return of land to our people, who are working toward teaching our children their true history, to make tomorrow a better world. And so, we must take heart that we are not powerless, that, indeed, we are as powerful as we think we are, and we must operate under that guiding premise. *Doneh ho.*

APPALACHIA, DEMOCRACY, AND CULTURAL EQUITY

Dudley Cocke

A joke from the Depression goes: Two Black men are standing in a government breadline; one turns to the other, "How you making it?" The other looks up the line, "White folks still in the lead."

Although central Appalachia's population is 98 percent white, the region joins the South Bronx, Bedford-Stuyvesant, and the Mississippi Delta at the bottom of the barrel in United States per capita income and college-educated adults. Two out of five students who make it to high school drop out before graduating, which is the worst dropout rate in the nation. Forty-two percent of the region's adults are functionally illiterate. In eastern Kentucky's Letcher County, half the children are classified as economically deprived, and almost a third of the area's households exist on less than $10,000 a year. What's the story here? Why are these white people doing so poorly? Part of the answer lies in the beginnings of the nation.

In the ascendancy of antidemocratic ideas such as those expressed by Alexander Hamilton and the Federalists were buried some of the the seeds of Appalachia's poverty. In opposition to Thomas Jefferson, Hamilton proposed that the president and

---

This article is based on presentations given in 1989, 1990, and 1991 at a series of Cultural Diversity Based on Cultural Grounding conferences and follow-up meetings.

Senate be elected for life; he wrote: "All communities divide themselves into the few and the many. The first are the rich and well-
born, the other the mass of people. The voice of the people has been
said to be the voice of God; and however generally this maxim has
been quoted and believed, it is not true in fact. The people are tur-
bulent and changing; they seldom judge or determine right." In
the next 200 years, this old-world idea would be cultivated by the
few for profit.

Capitalism didn't arrive in central Appalachia until the 1890's
(coinciding with the official closing of the western frontier). Before
then there were no banks, no railroads, and no industry on the
Cumberland Plateau. Monopoly capitalism arrived late and with a
vengeance. Timber and mineral rights were snapped up by absentee corporations for a fraction of their market value. Within twenty-five years, these corporations dominated the region's economy,
controlling the land, the labor pool, and the county courthouse.

Now, a hundred years later, central Appalachia is a mineral
colony of national and supranational energy corporations. Now the
region avoids at its own further peril international savvy. Union
Carbide was responsible for small chemical leaks in Institute, West
Virginia, as well as for the tragedy in Bhopal, India, in 1984. A
recent American appointee to the British Coal Board was partially responsible for the destruction of a Mingo County, West Virginia-
Pike County, Kentucky, community during the bitter 1984 to 1986
A.T. Massey coal strike. At the time of the strike, A.T. Massey was
a subsidiary of Royal Dutch Shell, which also mines in South
Africa. These absentee corporations, often with only a pretense of
national interest, continue to carry off Appalachia's wealth, leaving behind unemployment, poor schools, poor health care—in sum,
the poverty that Appalachia has come to represent.

A story points to how confusing poverty is to those who are
poor and those who try to empathize with it. In 1964, President
Lyndon Johnson declared the war on poverty. As part of the national media's coverage of that domestic war, CBS produced
"Christmas in Appalachia." Charles Kuralt narrated: "Up on the
hill is the Pert Creek School. And up there on this one day is the
only sign in this hollow that it is Christmas in Appalachia." The
camera cut to half a dozen kids gathered around a coal stove

singing "Silent Night." After the broadcast, a little town in Virginia named Appalachia received so many pairs of shoes, simply addressed to "Appalachia, U.S.A.," that the mayor and his coworkers were being pushed out of city hall. As the story goes, when it looked like the jail would be filled up, leaving no room for meanness, a shoe-burning party was proclaimed by City Council. The town helped rid the nation of its extra shoes and then returned to the routine of daily dealing with its lot.

Stereotyping has been a modus operandi consistently used by the relatively few to rationalize dominating the region's people and resources for profit. The inevitable missionaries, for example, chimed in with a chorus that had been singing since the early 1700's. In this instance, Marie Louise Poole opined in 1901: "Sometimes, unknown by them, I get a glimpse into their minds, and I am sick. There is filth in their thoughts. I want to save them." In 1912, the *New York Times* editorialized: "The majority of mountain people are unprincipled ruffians. There are two remedies only: education or extermination. The mountaineer, like the red Indian, must learn this lesson." Arnold Toynbee, in *A Study of History* (1935), writes by report, never having spent time in Appalachia: "The Appalachian mountain people at this day are no better than barbarians. They are the American counterparts of the latter-day White barbarian of the Old World, the Rifis and Kurds and the Hairy Ainu." The irony here is that the Ainu, who are people from the northernmost Japanese islands, have light skin, Caucasian features, and hairy bodies—we can imagine what some of the Japanese thought of them. The effect of this entrenched stereotyping has been to undermine a people's self-esteem.

In this demoralizing and divisive process, racism also has played its part: "They are of good stock. . . . They will overflow from their mountains, offset some unpromising foreign elements —and reinforce the nation," proclaimed Teddy Roosevelt. "In my opinion they are worse than the colored," remarked a Chicago police captain in a 1958 *Harper's* Magazine article. In the workplace, it was common practice for white coal operators to pit Black workers against Appalachia's white miners—and both against immigrant workers. For example, agents were sent to the deep South covertly to offer Black sharecroppers a rail ticket and a job up North in the mines. The new miners weren't told when they were being recruited as scab labor by the company to break the nascent union. After a while in many coal camps, it became company policy to keep, in their phrase, "a judicious mixture" of races and ethnicities, each group living separately and each speaking a different native tongue.

Given the despairing economic and social history in central Appalachia during the past 100 years, it is not unusual for someone to say, "Why don't you people just pick up and leave?" Almost always the tone implies, "After all, you are white." In the 1960's some of the absentee corporate owners, with input from the Army Corps of Engineers, sketched out such a plan: The region would be declared an energy preserve, a national sacrifice zone, and all but the necessary work force would be relocated. Especially for Appalachians with Indian blood, the plan had a familiar ring: In 1838, Cherokees turned to the mountains to hide their children from the forced march west—the Trail of Tears.

The leaving proposition also presumes that there is somewhere to go. When the coal and timber industries arrived after the Civil War, many families did pick up and move west to the Ozarks and then into Indian Territory, when it was taken back from the Indians. Or they scattered to other diminishing frontiers to pursue freedom. This marked migration of the 1890's dispels the then popular, economically convenient stereotype that Appalachian people were stuck in their hollows, too ignorant to find their way out—too dumb to discover progress. Throughout the boom and bust coal cycles of the past 100 years, tens of thousands of Appalachians have come and gone, often moving to industry jobs in cities like Flint, Michigan, coming back to visit regularly, despite more time spent driving than visiting, and coming home to be buried. Flint is not an option any longer. Neither is the frontier. In the face of ongoing hardship, many Appalachian people are determined to stay in their adopted homeland. In order to have a homeland to stay in, however, Appalachians will have to become less confused and more self-reliant.

There are signs of stiffening resistance to domination. During the 1990 United Mine Workers of America-Pittston coal strike, the union borrowed the Civil Rights Movement's strategy of massive nonviolent resistance, and Jesse Jackson's speeches were cheered by thousands of white miners, their families and supporters. Citizens' groups in numerous counties in the past several years have nixed plans for new waste dumps (New Jersey already buries 16 percent of its garbage in Kentucky). Now, for the first time in 100 years, corporate property taxes on unmined mineral wealth in eastern Kentucky are about to be assessed at something like full value. In 1988, by an overwhelming 80 percent, the voters amended the state constitution to outlaw the hated Broad Form Deed, which gave corporate mineral rights precedence over individual owner's surface rights. And in 1989, the Kentucky Supreme Court ruled the State's public school system unconstitutional because of its inequity.

Such victories in a one-industry economy are threatened, however, at every turn. Some argue that it is too little, too late. In less than a decade, mechanization has reduced the mining workforce by 30-plus percent, and the supranational corporations are looking to cheaper labor and more abundant coal in faraway places like China. More and more, Appalachia appears to be less the exception than the national norm: Many communities now find themselves playing host to businesses that have little sense of community responsibility and are owned by someone somewhere else. The paradigm of domination rests on what is proving daily to be a tragic misperception: that the interests and welfare of the few are more important than the interests and welfare of the many. To wit, the 1980's saw the greatest shift in wealth in the history of the United States: The bottom 20 percent of the American people on the economic ladder have lost 9 percent of their income, while the top 2 percent have gained 29 percent more income. Now, we find ourselves with a millionaire president, Cabinet, Congress, and media. If they are not millionaires themselves, they owe their office to great wealth. There now exists what Appalachia knows all too well and what Thomas Jefferson—who, nominally at least, stood for a broad-based democracy reliant on the will and consent of the majority of the people—likely feared the most: an almost perfect confluence of wealth and power. Is not such a plutocracy as odious as the monarchy of King George?

For many Appalachians, it has been acutely embarrassing to

be poor and white. But the fact is, Appalachia never has been white-white. Central Appalachia, with its rugged terrain of mountains, was one of the last pockets of the U.S. frontier. For such people as the Cherokee, it was hunting grounds of virgin forest. For a hundred years, runaway slaves made their way up the Appalachian chain toward the Susquehanna and the promise of freedom. Daniel Boone roamed thereabouts along with those relatively few hardy folk who chose to pursue their happiness away from civilization and get by on wild game, subsistence farming, barter, and herbal remedies. Many of these first frontiersmen and women were of Scotch-Irish descent. Today Appalachians hear themselves in their African-derived banjos, still eat their native corn bread and poke salad, and occasionally doctor themselves with herbal remedies. Scotch-Irish is not the only blood that flows in our veins. Those white Americans who are not making an effort to come to terms with the fact that they do not live in a white-white world, nation, or community are not realistic.

Appalachia's struggle for change in the nineties must continue to center itself in its communities, where the problems are tangible and one can get a grip on the solutions. One by one Appalachian communities must extricate themselves from the debility of feeling inferior, the morass of dependency, the divisiveness of blaming someone else, the slavery of trickle down. Self-reliance must be bolstered all around: economically, politically, and culturally. In this struggle, one hopes that each community will not sell itself short, but aspire to the highest ideals that its citizens can imagine. In so doing, a community will have to risk its insecurities and sensitivities by implicating itself in the wrongs that it has perpetuated and allowed to happen to itself. Only then can we have something like a second American revolution, and only then will it be possible for us to be a freer and happier people. One ringing lesson of this quincentenary from an historical perspective is that democracy is an arduous, sometimes fearful undertaking, and that the alternative is servitude.

DEMOCRACY'S CULTURAL CORRELATIVE: CULTURAL EQUITY

To move toward a paradigm of cultural equity, those in the dominant order—and I suspect that there is a part of all of us here in that—those of us with one foot in the dominant order can help move us toward such a paradigm by giving up the terms of domination. What are some of these terms? Domination's definitions are linear, hierarchical, top down, trickle down, done to. Equity's terms are circular, nonhierarchical, all around, done by. Domination calls for exclusion; equity values inclusion. Domination creates dependence; equity independence and self-reliance. Listen to their respective educational terms: to train him, to teach her; in contrast to building and sharpening one another—the South African concepts expressed in the Bantu *uakana* and *uglolana*. The paradigm of domination places efficiency (profit) before participation, product before process, mobility before attachment to place, the man-made order before the natural (and spiritual) worlds. It makes claims of objectivity, criticizing others for being too subjective. In the arts, it pretends to value formalistic concerns before concerns of content, because it takes its content of domination as a given. This has the effect of placing beauty (the beauty of domination) before issues of morality (leading directly to art for art's sake).

Finally, the paradigm of domination causes a hardship for the individual, because the paradigm doesn't really value most individuals. (To different degrees, this has proven true in both capitalist and socialist systems.) At best, within this paradigm of domination most individuals experience mild and regular disorientation, a sense of dislocation; at worst, a feeling of invisibility, in which they finally may be unable to perceive even themselves—a kind of walking death. Always, the paradigm of domination puts us at some (evolutionary) distance from being full human beings.

Let me emphasize that a new paradigm of equity would not rely on the *either/or* quality of my description. The desired synthesis, in dialectical terms, will be characterized by *both/and*. Thus, in our new paradigm we will not lose the usefulness of the straight line to the circle, objectivity to subjectivity, beauty to morality, disorientation as a way toward orientation. What will have changed is our conception of these terms, because our conception of ourselves and the world will have changed to make a new pattern of meaning. A paradigm that values neighborliness and peace and restores the primacy of the common good is what I believe we should be working for. If we could but see it, this is in our self-interest.

Appalshop and Roadside Theater, where I work in Appalachia, attempt to operate out of something like this kind of paradigm. This effort is reflected in our collective organizational structure and in our goal to make films, television, music recording, radio, and theater that are relative to the region's daily life.

Exactly how do we, then, make our work? Most all of Appalshop's people were born in the region; all have an allegiance to the working class. Roadside has developed both an indigenous performance style and an indigenous body of plays by drawing on its heritages of storytelling, balladry, oral histories, and church. The community participates in the creation of new plays first as resource for the script and later as respondent and critic during the various stages of play development. Some of our productions incorporate local talent in the performance event. When completed, the production is performed throughout the region—in churches, community centers, outdoor amphitheaters, wherever people come together. The play is often the occasion for community discussion.

Likewise, if we are making a half-hour television show about the high cancer rate of those drinking the water from Yellow Creek, Kentucky, we make the show as a coproduction with that part of the Yellow Creek community concerned with the problem. Thus the television show not only informs a broad, five-state regional audience (and sometimes a national audience) through broadcast, it also provides the host community with an organizing tool.

And what, then, when the work travels out, as it very often does? We are constantly devising ways for our context to travel out with us. Poet Marianne Moore remarked that people don't like what they don't understand. Roadside believes that it must provide the opportunities, in as many ways as it can, to that understanding. Wherever we go, we make a special effort to invite working-class and rural people to our events.

Crossing cultural boundaries is not like attending a cocktail party with strangers. It is more like being brought into a family circle. It is an intimate experience that requires patience and respect. It takes time. Fifteen or so years ago, an internationally famous folksinger from California came to the mountains to perform in the county's high-school auditorium. A big crowd was on hand as a local string band opened the concert. The band held the audience's rapt attention. The famous folksinger followed with some success. Backstage, she made a point to congratulate the local band on their performance, noting that she, too, often sang from the same Appalachian repertoire. She went on to say how keenly the audience had been listening to their music and wondered what their secret was. "What is that little something extra you seem to have?" she asked emphatically. She pressed for an answer. Finally the fiddle player spoke up, "Well ma'am, the only difference that I could tell was that you were playing out front of them ol' songs, and we were right behind them."

The final measure for Appalshop's work is the health of our community, the well-being of our people. Appalshop's role is to nurture a creative discourse with its tradition. In such a way we hope to help our community meet the challenge of the present and prepare for the future.

Culture, and art as one of its potent expressions, is fundamental to our we-ness. Without our stories and songs, paintings and sculpture, we have difficulty recognizing ourselves. To deny a people their cultural expression is to deny them their existence. This is why oppressed people cling so tenaciously to their cultural practices. It is why their art is often encoded, its power and meaning hidden behind screens through which only those in solidarity can pass. One fears loss, dilution, cooptation. Culture carries a people's profound expression of their self-hood. Only when peoples can meet as equals, without the threat of domination, can they risk their art and culture. Cultural equity, then, is integral to democracy and the making of an American people from our many diverse strands.

Appalachia's culture, like the majority of North America's more than one hundred identifiable cultures, is not now accorded this equity, respect, and right to self-determination. A large tan-

gle of Appalachia's roots reach back to western Europe, and especially to the British Isles. There, too, it is the grand tradition, what
has become the art of the few, that presently rules. The fact that
most American cultures have living links with artistic traditions
in other parts of the world is a compelling argument for international exchange—and a reason for most of us to offer ourselves as
students before our continent's Native peoples, whose roots here
have the benefit of ten thousand years of cultivation.

Corazones / rostros	Hearts / faces
Corazones / rostros	*Hearts / faces*
Amerindios	*Amerindian*
Suenos	*Dreams*
Tiran raices en los suelos	*Casting roots in the earth*
Tienden ramas en cielos	*Spreading branches in the sky*

—*Alurista*

INDIGENISMO

THE CALL TO UNITY

Amalia Mesa-Bains, Ph.D.

The multicultural discourse grows confused and often falters on the issues of language, terminology, and naming. As the mainstream institutions attempt to appropriate multicultural themes, the descriptions of race, ethnicity, and nationality grow more euphemistic. In such a context cultural groups must struggle for specificity in their self-representation against the vague homogeneity imposed by a dominant society.

Consequently, in the "Hispanic debate," the term *Chicano* echoes as a self-description of the historical, political, and cultural references of the largest group within the greater Latino communities of the United States. The Chicano experience provides a fertile ground for examining the critical issues of identity, origin, history, ancestry, affiliation, and activism.

This paper was developed as a result of the Cultural Diversity Based on Cultural Grounding Conference in 1989 in New York City and follow-up meetings in 1990 and 1991.

Looking back at the 1960s and early 70s Chicano experience, there is often the tendency to describe the involvement with Indian identity issues as a neoindigenous effort. The neoindigenous is seen as simply a mythologizing aspect of the formation of Chicano identity. Rather, I think it is important to explore *Indigenismo* as a central foundation for both personal and collective identities formed in activism. For those of us engaged in that historic period known as *el movimiento,* the Chicano Movement was a time of self-definition inspired by a sense of injustice and by hope for fairer treatment. Part of this struggle meant giving voice to an identity of our own making. The discriminatory treatment we endured as Mexicans had made it quite clear to us that the Anglo society did not regard us as white, and it insured our desire not to be identified as white. For the Chicano, to be nonwhite meant to be Indian. Consequently, the issues were not so much of racial ambiguity and designation as they were of cultural choice. How this indigenous identity was fashioned was as much a function of the meaning of our groups and their leadership as it was a personal endeavor. Recouping this indigenous activism for a new generation of Chicanos forming their identity in a historical discourse requires us to engage in critical narratives.

It is to these issues that this paper is dedicated.

In a period of historic demographic change, the Latino community has become the fastest-growing ethnic group in the United States, well beyond 20 million members and soon to be the major Latino group in the Southwest. Yet, despite this startling growth, Chicanos cannot presume that majority status will indicate commensurate sociopolitical power in society. The Chicano as a Mexican-descended American continues to struggle against socioeconomic marginalization, educational failure, political disenfranchisement and media distortion. Survival and transformation within these circumstances requires that the Chicano community strengthen its central identity and engage in resourceful practices. Such a rededication to sustaining values and identities calls for a rethinking of past Chicano beliefs and a consideration of their significance to contemporary conditions.

The early Chicano Movement and its organizing principles are currently being examined in cultural criticism. Looking at the history of practices and beliefs about collective Chicano identity can bring us insights into the central role of Indian ancestry and indigenous experiences. This period of retrospection and redefinition will contribute to the ongoing invention of Chicano identity for the twenty-first century.

Our cultural identity has been based on core spiritual, mythic, ancestral, and historical-political beliefs. For many cultural workers, artists, and scholars engaged in community practices of resistance and affirmation, the remembrance of these beliefs was an inspiration for social action.

A vanguard of artists, activists, and intellectuals was instrumental in articulating a cultural identity based on the experiences and needs of the larger Mexicano-Americano population in the United States. This vanguard, formed in the crucible of the Chicano Movement of the 1960s and '70s, has, over the last twenty-five years, established community institutions and directed areas of study and service framed by guiding beliefs. Within this larger movement, Chicanos in California took leadership in the development of Amerindian thought. This paper will examine these conceptual foundations and these early institutions within a historical perspective and toward a contemporary application.

Only as a flower is man honored upon earth;
an instant so brief he enjoys the flower of spring;
rejoice with them! I am saddened.

I come from the house of the delicate butterflies;
my song unfolds her petals:
behold these myriad flowers;
my heart is a motley painting.

— *Nahuatl poem*

I. PALABRAS

The need to affirm our own cultural reality through our resistance to exploitation and our experience as an internally colonized community within the United States was a driving force in the numerous fronts of the Chicano Movement. Whether in response to farmworkers' conditions, land and water rights struggles, bilingual education needs, or in the largest sense of redress for an historical presence long denied, Chicano activism sought to link social demands with cultural expression. The new Chicano culture was rooted in an Amerindian, or indigenous, American heritage. Spiritual and humanitarian values distilled from Toltec, Mayan, Aztec, and other ancient cultures were integrated with the militant traditions of *La Raza,* or the people. The ability to reclaim the ancient legacy through contemporary devices of invention was a key factor in creating a collective identity. The vibrancy of an indigenous Chicano world view became a profound intellectual and artistic current of the period.

This language of the indigenous brought a conceptual base to the Chicano Movement. Although most influential in California, Amerindian issues were also reflected in other regions. Reclaiming an indigenous ancestry helped forge an oppositional identity, which could contest and resist the domination of the larger society. Chicanos used this strong indigenous philosophy to criticize the materialism of Anglo society. As Jorge Klor de Alva describes:

> It was only when dramatic transformations in ideology seemed desirable and possible that many Chicanos countered Anglo ethics, metaphysics, and logic with Mexican indigenous philosophy.[1]

Consequently, the conceptual base of Chicano thinking absorbed elements from various pre-Hispanic cultures, in particular, the philosophic and religious basis was reappropriated in the inventive manner characteristic of Chicano cultural practices. Artists and writers selected fragments of philosophy that were useful, often extending meanings to suit the situations, even mixing concepts from different groups and periods of ancient history. The works of Miguel Leon Portillo and Angel Garibay were essential to this effort. Old concepts were rearranged and repositioned in creative flexible devices to name, mark and link people, places, and beliefs culturally and politically. Often referred to as "mystico-militaristic," the terminology of indigenismo—the emphasis on positive values associated with Indian cultures—was a useful philosophy to empower Chicanos to unite and resist the exploitation of the majority society. The naming and marking processes in particular laid out a foundation myth, a point of origin, as well as a high point of cultural development and legacy. The Meso-American ancestry provided the Chicanos a sense of their own history of great civilizations that gave them the courage to defy in acts of political civil disobedience.

The widespread influence of Meso-American spirituality made constant references to spiritual unity, energy, and love, which referred to extensive Nahuan- and Mayan-inspired thought. The conceptual linking of such thought served as a very practical means of strengthening the demands for legitimate bilingual-bicultural education, fair labor wages and practices, and even redistribution of appropriated land. For Chicanos involved in sometimes violent confrontations with the police and other legal authorities in defense of their communities, the beliefs of the pre-Hispanic world were inspirational and provided psychic strength in a battle for human rights.

In the 1960s, an era when the new identity of Chicanos was being formed, it was essential to describe a historic past, long denied in American society, in relationship to a set of sustaining beliefs. It was fundamental in order to contest contemporary Anglo values and to protect historic Mexican descendedness to identify with Meso-American philosophies about land, art, and even the after-life. As Tomas Ybarra-Frausto reminds us, major Chicano leaders:

asked for the revitalization of an indigenous Chicano world view as an antidote to the vacuous and sterile reality of white America. . . Chicanos [were] admonished to absorb the human-itarian and spiritual values of the Indian heritage as elements contributing, now, in the present, to a symbolic new birth. [And] to question the modern loss of venerable customs.[2]

The act of revitalizing required more than language or terminolo-gy. It required an ideological-conceptual base that could remain flexible and responsive to changing needs of the group. Chicanos, long affiliated with Catholic iconography and religious symbols, had to throw off many of these European-dominated elements, yet still find ways to blend, in a syncretic fashion, historical symbols of unity, faith, passion, and hope into the new collective identity being formed. So a figure like the Virgen de Guadalupe was also called Tonantzin, or Great Mother, in the Nahuatl language. In this way, Meso-American thought could serve as a model of ideas while also functioning as a model for an imaginative act of memory linking the discontinuous and fragmented past to the transformation of the future. American Indian practices of organizing, which were so tied to their identity and cultures, became a model for Chicanos struggling to clarify their own Indian identity and address their dire social conditions. Such identity models, which gave Chicanos our only tie to an ancient history, helped strengthen the developing Chicano cultural interventions on behalf of the community. Thus, Chicano culture reflects a third set of cultural values, not completely Mexican and decidedly non-Anglo. This development called for the invention of an identity crystallized from key experiences that had more than one cultural meaning. These cultural values were concerned with defining aspects of the community that could effectively counter exploitation and disenfranchisement. Thus concepts, language, naming, marking, spirituality, and self-representation were all critical to a connectedness that linked Chicanos through flexible networks within the United States.

> *I am Cuauhtemoc*
> *Proud and noble*
> *leader of men*
>
> *I am the Maya Prince*
> *I am Nezahualcoyotl*
> *Great leader of the Chichimecas*
>
> *I am the Eagle and Serpent of*
> *the Aztec Civilization*
> > *—Rudolfo "Corky" Gonzales*

Naming: Self: Xicano

The naming process in particular was a device of opposition to the larger North American culture. *Chicano*, as a term, was believed to be a shorthand form of *Mexicanos* (pronounced *Mechicanos*, from *Mechicas* of Tenochtitlan), which was taken as a self-representation in opposition to the Eurowestern emphasis on Spanish heritage. It was also a negative slang term, now reversed to identify a positive cultural reality. The term *Xicanos* (pronounced *shicanos*, to be used as an indigenous spelling of *Chicanos*), then, reflected a position of political resistance to ethnic stereotyping, discrimination, and political repression. Ironically, this redefinition based on indigenous ancestry came after years of bureaucratic attempts by such groups as the United League of Latin Americans (LUCAC) to remove Mexicans from a U.S. Census designation as Indians to a designation as Hispanic Europeans. The contradiction of a new generation disillusioned with acculturation and in search of their Indian past was modeled on the Black nationalist and Pan-Africanist movements of African Americans. The Xicano identity reclaimed the Meso-American past by calling attention to the annihilation of great civilizations, which resulted from catastrophic genocide in the New World, and it even challenged the authority of the "primitive savage" myth, which had been the legacy of those historic events. As a term, *Xicano* set apart a new generation of Mexican-descended people who could be proud of an ancestry with a glorious past. Xicano was a call to self based on two interrelated positions: resistance to the exploitative Anglo society and affirmation of Mexican cultural values and everyday barrio life.

Naming: Place: Aztlan

The earliest Xicano identity was framed in a resistance to the debilitating, racist, and limited values of the dominant culture and affirmed a *mestizaje*, or blend, of Indian and Spanish blood, based on an indigenist core. Such a world view maintained a complex system of ancestry, territory, and mythology founded in the continent. The term *Aztlan*, derived from the Nahuatl *Aztatlan* (meaning *place of the herons*), was interpreted by Xicanos as the lands to the north. Thus the Xicano perspective grew to signifiy Mexico's northern empire, or the Southwest. Film scholar Chon A. Noriega described the concept of Aztlan, the mythical homeland of the Aztecs and the reclaimed nationhood of Chicanos, in 1969:

> By 1965, diverse social protests in the Southwest had coalesced into a national civil rights movement known as the Chicano Movement. Aztlan—now considered its fundamental ideological construct or living myth—provided an alternative geography for these efforts to reclaim, reform, or redefine social space—land,

government, schools, and the urban barrio. Aztlan also helped
set in motion a cultural reclamation project in literature, the
arts, scholarships and everyday culture and in its current sense,
Aztlan now refers to those places where Chicano culture flour-
ishes.[3]

This symbolic term, *Aztlan*, is indicative of the emphases on reclamation that anchored Chicano identity. Despite the contradictory
Mexican history of Indian conquests and *mestizo* resistance, Aztlan
became what Noriega describes as "a complex geopolitical space."

The notion of a complex geopolitical space has multiple references for Xicanos. The history of Mexicans is marked by the
internal colonization of a people isolated from the remaining
Mexican nation by the United States annexation of 1848
(Guadalupe Hidalgo Treaty). This colonial appropriation of 51 percent of Mexico's land followed the already historic loss of original
Meso-American earth to the earliest Spanish *conquistadores*.
These dual memories of loss had marked the Xicano psyche with
an abiding need for a homeland and a point of origin in that territory. Aztlan served as this territorial point of rebirth.

Writers and poets were the prime originators and exponents
of the Amerindian concept of Aztlan. In particular the Xicano poet
Alurista synthesized a Xicano identity that fused ancient spiritual languages or beliefs with elements of Mexican day-to-day barrio realities. His work infused Xicano nationalism with a
mytho-spiritual dimension. The self construction of Xicano identity was a collective phenomenon rooted in group life and needs.
The Meso-American or Amerindian origin was the core around
which aspects of *Mexicanidad*, or urban barrio styles, and other
cultural elements were organized. An ongoing process of community activism produced cultural images that were depicted by
artists. Equally significant to the spread of a unifying indigenismo was the development of cultural arts centers, or *centros*, and
their leadership. The combination of artists and centros, linked
with the vanguard of student leaders, established a common spiritual language and iconography.

Naming: People: La Raza Cosmica or La Nueva Raza

At the most extended level, the group naming was expanded to include all Mexican-descended people and made use of earlier concepts established by Mexico's historic philosopher of the 1920s and 1930s, Jose Vasconcellos, whose term *La Raza Cosmica* referred also to the idea of a new people. The cosmic dimension was in keeping with the Xicano concept of a new or invented identity. Vasconcellos's notion of contributions of great indigenous civilizations blended with the Spanish cultural element was recast by Xicanos to emphasize the indigenous lineage. La Nueva Raza, the newborn people, or reborn youth, was also part of the linking language that could embrace communities and activists across the Southwest, fostering inclusive definitions of peoplehood. Consequently, naming of place/Aztlan, naming of self/Xicano, and naming of peoples/La Raza Cosmica or La Nueva Raza were part of a continuous reappropriation of selected elements of mytho-spiritual meaning, fused with militant social demands that could suit contemporary needs.

Within this development of spiritual ideology, the *Plan Espiritual de Aztlan*, forged from a 1969 youth conference in Denver, stands, in retrospect, as a constitutional moment for Xicanos. Derived from concepts of nationhood, the Plan was envisioned to speak of beliefs and philosophy and to set goals and direction, which could and would inspire a generation. Key statements centered on rights to land reclamation:

> The land belongs to those who plant the seeds, water the fields and gather the crops, not to foreign Europeans.[4]

This emphasis on a non-white, working-class identity was strengthened by an association with other Native groups. A vanguard of Xicanos solidified their connection to American Indian struggles, which provided examples of self-determination. Xicanos were influenced by the Latin American Indianist Movement's position on culture, which emphasized creating an awareness of the conditions and needs of overlooked segments of the population and presenting Indian cultures as expressions of a civilization opposed to European values.[5] The alliance of contemporary Xicano-Indian communities was an inevitable outgrowth of a commonly suffered exploitation.

The awareness of the historical Mexican colonization of American Indian groups such as the Yaquis compelled Xicanos in California to attempt to heal the divisions by identifying with historical figures of resistance in Apache, Comanche, and Yaqui communities. Early associations of artists, activists, and intellectuals were often based on common memories of Manifest Destiny, which had been disastrous for Indian and Mexican alike. Among the memorable aspects of these Xicano-Indian alliances were the Pan-Indian occupation of Alcatraz in California. The development of D-Q University from 1970 to 1978 as an Indian-Xicano educational institution was reflected in its name, a fusion of the names of Deganwidah, the leader of the Iroquois Confederacy, and Quetzacoatl, the Toltec deity.

The Academia of La Nueva Raza, a Xicano-Indian collective of artists and intellectuals in New Mexico, maintained a commitment to a shared struggle of the Indian-Xicano communities in publications, conferences, and exhibits, including work with the Tricentennial Commission of the All-Indian Pueblo Council. In regions of the Southwest, particularly New Mexico and Arizona, the contact and day-to-day alliances between Pueblo Indians and Xicanos fostered some common political activism, while long-standing traditions, such as the *Conchero*, or Mexican ritual dancers, used music, dance, and poetry to link Xicanos to ongoing Indian life.

Throughout the foundational period of cultural self-construction, Xicanos reappropriated sources, formed Xicano-Indian partnerships, and gave voice to elements of their indigenous heritage. Naming, marking, and linking with the symbolic and social realities of an Amerindian culture gave the Xicano Movement a spiritual base for its political and economic goals.

> *I, Nezahualcoyotl ask this question:*
> *Is it true that one lives with roots on earth?*
> *Not to remain on earth forever; only a short while.*
>
> *Even if it's made of gold it breaks.*
> *Even if it's made of quetzal feathers it's torn.*
> *Not to be on earth forever, only for a short while.*
> —*Nezahualcoyotl*

Naming: Artist: Tolteca

The role of the artist as both creator and activist came, in some part, from idealized Xicano interpretations of Toltec culture. The concept of an artist-statesman, as well as an interdisciplinary arts model, emphasized a central role for artists, poets, and musicians. The artist-statesman, the *Tolteca*, was responsible for interpreting ancient cultural practices and creating a new ethos. The formulation of the artist's work was influenced by Nahuatl religious writings, which guided Xicanos philosophically. Discipline, spirituality, aesthetics, and social purpose were influenced by ancient models elaborated in writings by Miguel Leon Portillo and other pre-Columbianists.

For a generation of artists struggling against models of exclusivity and images of Anglo male art production, the Tolteca way was a set of inspirational beliefs. This concept of the artist-statesman was in keeping with the new Xicano charge of the artist as an agent of social change. Prevailing Xicano convictions included the concept that art that would give form to social conscience and be driven by progressive humanist traditions. The emphasis on collective activities encouraged artistic production responsive to group values. The development of skills in the visual and performing arts and in writing and oratory was an ideal for many Xicano cultural workers aiming at the artist-statesman role reminiscent of ancient civilizations.

Particular leader figures in the Meso-American past were inspirations for the construction of the Xicano artist's role. Quetzalcoatl—the god-man as lawgiver, spiritual source, statesman, and visionary—and Nezahualcoyotl, the poet-king, were both major figures in the Tolteca concept that influenced Xicanos. These philosophical positions were integrated with the militaristic function of community self-defense. The Xicanos then could be guided internally by a sense of lineage that included both warrior and artist. These two roles coincided with the stances of resistance and affirmation. As the Xicano Movement created a commitment to anti-elitist, publicly accessible cultural expression, Xicanos had to refashion the divine-monarch-as-artist concept into practices that would serve a popular need. For cultural workers other deities were also essential to popularizing such symbolic meaning—

Ometeotl, embodying the dual principle of self-creation; Tonantz-in-Cuatlique, Mother Earth, and Tezcatlipoca, brother to Quetzalcoatl, invisible god of the night sun. Reflecting the powers of creation and transformation, these figures were often represented in both visual imagery and in literary texts.

The Xicano identity constituted itself through reclaiming elements of the ancestral past, while consolidating them in light of the need to counter an often hostile contemporary society. Consequently, establishing the base of belief with a strong indigenist center prepared the cultural worker to transform words into deeds. Imaginative acts of memory have provided Xicanos a link to ancestry and history in times of loss, separation, and suppression. It has been through these acts of memory that redemption has been possible.

> *It is not the great plumed serpent*
> *that we seek in the dark and lonely*
> *niches of the street. We seek the mysteries*
> *of who we came to be. Victims*
> *of the prison of the skin*
> — *Felipe Campos Mendez*

II. OBRAS

We can say that the radical reclamation by Xicanos of concepts, languages, terminology and work roles of the Meso-American ancient world matched already existing popular practices, which melded a native world view about healing, an empahsis on a harmonious relationship with the natural world, and indigenous spirituality. The existence of this Amerindian stance was not just an artistic and intellectual reclamation, but rather a powerful testimony to day-to-day folk life below the surface of many Xicano communities. For example, Xicano life was often characterized by either first-hand experience of healing or family tales of miraculous cures. *Curanderismo,* or healing, has its foundation in a belief in the unity of body and mind. Herbs and other natural phenomena are used to heal physical illness as well as the psychic and emotional turmoil associated with it. In this case, not even the physical and psychic destruction that occurred in the Meso-American world could erase the cultural practices pertaining to healing, death, and ceremony. The wholistic nature of curanderismo is present in popular attitudes about health and wellness. Historic and legendary healers like Don Pedrito Jaramillo of South Texas used healing practices involving herbs, talismans, and water, which included the family members in the cure. Healing and the use of family altars was strongest in Texas and other border areas, and artists-cultural workers like Carmen Lomas Garza and Santa Barraza depicted these indigenous practices in their prints and paintings. A *curandera*, or healer, would diagnose an individual and might administer a *limpia*, or cleansing, with smoke, rolling an egg over the body, or removing bad spirits through the ear with a burning funneled paper. The artistic images reinforced the family's belief in collective healing.

The extensive evidence of home altars in family life in many parts of the Southwest also attests to Amerindian spiritual antecedents. Home altars have come to function as history-keeping structures for Xicanos, who dutifully record the births, deaths, separations, miraculous interventions, and life events in the narrative of their family life. Indigenous elements are mixed with saintly icons; and Africanic practices from herbal botanicas further reflect the heterogeneity of indigenous experience. The use of sage or copal as a cleansing herb or of curative *polvos*, or powders, and images of Guadalupe-Tonantzin operate side by side in the altars. Infused with other longstanding indigenous practices, Xicano spirituality also bears traces of Meso-American beliefs regarding death. In border regions, the Mexican-descended tradition of *Dia de los Muertos*, the Day of the Dead, has permeated the Xicano's innovative uses of gravesite decorations and home *ofrendas*, or altars. Also persistent are beliefs about the return of the spirits of the dead from the land of *Mictlan* (place of the dead) and constituent elements characteristic of death offerings. Special foods, drink, icons, folk forms, song, and storytelling demonstrate the function of memory in maintaining an indigenous presence within contemporary Xicano community life. The emphasis on the ephemeral, the commitment to ancestral honor, and the contestatory struggle for life against day-to-day poverty and exploitation are characteristics of indigenismo that are key to the Xicano identity.

The reclamation of indigenous consciousness required Xicanos to synthesize new *ceremonias* (ceremonies). These ceremonias were specific spectacles used to induce the transformative state of the Tolteca through *danza* (dance), sweats, or purifications in communal activities. Xicanos used this mixture of Amerindian practices with the aim of preparing the artist to serve the community with respect and commitment. Visiting Mexican Conchero and *Matachine* dancers provided knowledge that included an evolving study of homeopathy, prayer, poetry, meditation, and dance for men and women. In total, Xicano artists were reclaiming pre-Hispanic scholarship, defining their own popular practices, and reconnecting with the traditional artisans of Mexico.

Key to this integration of indigenous forces were the tactical and strategic devices of selection, reclamation, and preservation of the knowledge and cultural acts essential to combatting the oppressive stance of the larger society. In this way Xicano artists creatively reappropriated those indigenous concepts, language, figures, and practices that could be of service to the community. Xicanos were never in search of a comprehensive reconstruction of pre-Hispanic life. Instead they preferred to inventively make use of strategic meanings—fusing and mixing them in a creative manner essential to community strengthening and self-defense. Aztec warrior concepts of sacrifice and dedication were employed to sustain resistance to police harassment, exploitation, and incarceration. These warrior concepts were balanced by earth-mother figures, the Tonantzins, which were emblematic of healing. These ancient figures and practices were called upon in face of the staggering health and poverty emergencies experienced by working-class Xicanos. The appropriation of early Aztec imagery, such as Cuahtemoc the warrior, related to issues of self-defense, while Mayan deities and references were associated with demands for higher education. These tactical choices of ancestral images and deities were fundamental to Xicano Amerindian thought and language. Despite the Meso-American life decimated in the catastrophic invasion and occupation by the Spaniards, Xicanos, in their historic moment of rebirth, or *renacimiento*, recalled ancient pre-Hispanic cultures.

This combination of forces occurred during the most intense

period of Xicano student organizing, militant activism, and cultural synthesis—the late 1960's and early 1970's. Understandably this period has become the foundation for the groups, centers, and leadership that evolved from community need, regional uniqueness, and shared values. This section will look at work springing from the conceptual base of indigenismo within three major California *colectivas* (collectives), including Centro Cultural de la Raza/Los Toltecas de Aztlan, with Alurista in San Diego; the Teatro Campesino, with Luis Valdez in San Juan Bautista; and the Mujeres Muralistas, with Patricia Rodriguez and others in San Francisco.

Centro: Centro Cultural de la Raza, San Diego
Grupo: Los Toltecas de Aztlan
Tolteca: Alurista

The earliest formation of Los Toltecas de Aztlan in 1969 was a collective growing out of the leadership of several artists, including Victor Ocha, Guillermo Aranda, Salvador Roberto Torres, Mario Acevedo, and Alurista. The group's name reinforced the growing commitment to an indigenous approach to social identity and political activism. Los Toltecas was composed at one point of over forty men and women who were artists, musicians, poets, and dancers. This interdisciplinary *grupo*, or group, linked to indigenismo, used a philosophical approach that included studies of history, culture, cosmology, and mythology of pre-Hispanic Mexico and California, known as *Califas*.

Deeply attached to the notion of a centro for the community of San Diego, Los Toltecas created much of the first structure of that city's Centro Cultural de la Raza. The community's demand for a center eventually resulted in a real building after years of struggle and a militant stand in Chicano Park in the Logan Heights barrio. The water tower building in San Diego's Balboa Park became the home of Los Toltecas and Centro Cultural de la Raza in 1971. Alurista continued his classes, new danzante groups were formed to study Aztec, Conchero, and Nahuatl dances, and muralists like Victor Ocha used Pan-Indian imagery on the centro's outside walls. Many of the Toltecas strengthened ties to the indigenous issues of treaty rights and national sovereignty in solidarity with Pueblo groups like the Hopi.

A key figure in the formation of indigenous thought both nationally and locally was the Toltecan poet Alurista. He is widely credited as being a major participant in the formation of contemporary Amerindian ideology through his unique literary, linguistic, and cultural blending of Mexican indigenous heritage and barrio living. Alurista developed his work with Nahuatl-Mayan concepts and issues related to indigenous peoples of the Southwest, but also went on to emphasize broader Third World concerns. His fusion of militant political analysis with his understanding of ancient endurance is reflected in his beliefs about struggle:

> Where do we begin?...with the rifle or with the pen? With the armed revolt for the popular take-over of the Yankee state or with the cultural revolution for organization of the popular revolutionary conscience of the Chicano peoples north of Mexico. The first alternative is heroic suicide. The second is protracted (long-range) insurrection.[6]

Not satisfied with just the subject of indigenous knowledge, he turned to form, using the poetic, collective voice. He noted that unlike elite European poetic practices, Nahuatl poetry was publicly sung and collectively danced as much by the nobility as by the working class. In his progressive interpretation of community spectacle, Alurista contributed a major indigenous view that deepened the publicly accessible aspects of poetry. He maintained that one of the chief goals of the Xicano Movement was the creation of consciousness and change in the social and material environment, which went beyond an art that provided only aesthetic pleasure.

Alurista's specific application of various pre-Hispanic cultures reflected his deep understanding of the connections between thought and action, introspection and social activism. Of particular importance, as both Klor de Alva and Ybarra Frausto have noted, was his move from militaristic Nahuatl thought to Mayan aestheticism. His poetry gave language to a spirituality based on Mayan concepts such as cosmogonic energy, found in nature and in the self. These ideas provided symbolic images for courage, which were applied to Xicano issues. Alurista, perhaps more than any other Tolteca, finds philosophy and ideology inseparably linked to spirit and power. Once again the twin forces of affirmation and resistance guided the activism of the Xicano Movement. The significance of Alurista's contribution to the collective of Los Toltecas is clear and his importance to an integrated Amerindian element in Xicano identity unquestionable.

In the years since the growth of the Centro Cultural de la Raza, a new emphasis on border relations with Mexico as well as a continuous influx of Mexicano cultural resources has established the Centro in a pivotal position. The Centro supported the work of the Border Arts Workshop, particularly during the years of Guillermo Gomez-Pena's participation. Gomez-Pena sees the Xicano indigenismo as an aspect of an agenda for political unity and self-determination.

At that time what very few people understood about indigenismo was its innovative nature. By recognizing the Chicano conditions in light of that of American Indians, and by extension their Mexican compadres, the Concheros, they created the basis for true transcontinental consciousness at a grass-roots level. This consciousness didn't acknowledge the existence of the border or the European derived governments, and mainstream cultures of the U.S. and Mexico.[7]

Grupo: El Teatro Campesino, San Juan Bautista
Tolteca: Luis Valdez

Like Alurista, Luis Valdez also looked toward the philosophic foundation of the Meso-American world in the development of Teatro Campesino. From its earliest theatrical presentations on flatbed trucks in Delano, California—an innovation of the *carpa*, or tent theater, tradition—Teatro Campesino has had a strong conceptual language of indigenismo. Using practices and language strongly tied to a belief in a free *pueblo*, or community, Valdez was active in the Huelga Movement of the United Farmworkers' struggle for fair pay, decent working conditions, and an end to exploitation. In his work to broaden awareness of the conditions of farmworkers, Luis Valdez found the relationship between spirit and action. Reflecting on life beyond political and guerrilla theater, he says,

I think that the type of theater we must evolve must be scientific and religious. Not one that goes into mysticism and mystification, but instead brings into focus truth and how truth functions. If we continue on the cultural trends that we have followed as Chicanos we will encounter a Mayan system of thought that deals with these truths. The moment we reach out and understand these concepts we will cease to become just Chicanos, we will become human beings. Our theater will universalize the Chicano Movement.[8]

In his development of a theater philosophy based on Mayan thought, Valdez also pushed the aesthetic forms beyond the *actos*, or skits, of everyday struggle to embrace *mitos*, or ancestral myths as well. The two forms were to complement each other; Valdez describes *los actos y los mitos* as two visions of a universal reality—one through the eyes of man, the other through the eyes of God. Often using the Quetzalcoatl-Kulkan image of the plumed serpent, Valdez posited self-liberation through the understanding of ancestral legacy.

While expanding the original guerrilla theater to Xicano and Califas themes in plays like *Soldier Bay, Corridos* and *Zoot Suit*, El Teatro Campesino has maintained a tradition of spiritual religiosity that bears the indigenous mark. In its annual Virgen de Tepeyac Pageant, honoring la Virgen de Guadalupe, the company involves the local community as actors in the setting of the Mission of San Juan Bautista. The powerful Dia de los Muertos spectacle also presents the traditional ceremonies of the Amerindian world that are essential to the world view of the Teatro. Formed in the late 1960s, the Teatro continues through the committed work of the Valdez family, Phil Esparza, and a dedicated company. They remain anchored in the basic Mayan concepts of dynamic form and movement and universally apply them through the techniques of commedia dell'arte, music and dance theater, magic, realism, and sociopolitical theater. The duality of a campesino aesthetic and language rooted in a New World reality is the fundamental precept of El Teatro Campesino.

As a Tolteca Luis Valdez has been a leading figure—from his earliest role in the writing and editing of the Plan Espiritual of Aztlan in 1969, along with Alurista in the Xicano Movement, to his Mexican and international cultural exchanges. El Teatro Campesino's world tours have brought a better understanding of the Xicano's cultural grounding to wide audiences. Luis Valdez has integrated Meso-American thought into group structures, aesthetic forms, and visionary language. Like Alurista, he has challenged hierarchical mainstream practices by creating a more democratic art form with inclusive and participatory opportunities. Teatro Campesino's mixture of philosophic Meso-American meanings and vernacular language brought dignity and a human, universal essence to everyday life and struggle for the farm worker.

Grupo: Mujeres Muralistas, San Francisco
Toltecas: Patricia Rodriguez, Consuelo Mendez Castillo,
Irene Perez, and Graciela Carillo de Lopez

The consolidation of an indigenous world view for Xicanos relied not only on the language of poetry, music, dance, and theater, but also on the power of visual imagery. Both posters and murals were used to facilitate group formation. The Xicano mural movement was a critical aspect of the expressive arts that clarified identity issues through a public discourse. Murals served as a larger-than-life visual narrative connecting communities, telling missing histories, presenting cultural themes, reappropriating neighborhood space, and creating a new Xicano imagery. As a function of identity development, murals affirmed family roles, popular practices, indigenous spiritual beliefs, and political demands. Within this mural movement, collectives and brigades that sought to develop collaborative models and structures provided important leadership. This leadership was marked by the active presence of women.

The Mujeres Muralistas developed out of this collective context of grupos that emphasized nonelitist models. Because of differences with male muralists over mural content, the women formed their own collective to provide support for their women- and family-focused work. A significant part of this work was inspired by the indigenous experiences and heritage of the muralists. The representation of indigenous images that were not associated with warrior roles contributed to an expanded conceptual base for affirming indigenismo. The mural images, particularly *Latinoamerica*, commissioned in 1974 in San Francisco's Mission district, expanded a role for women. Emphasizing the traditions of native women from Mexico and Latin America, the mural reflected the collective's own Chicana Latina composition. As a result of the artists' relationships and heritage, as well as the pan-Latino nature of the Mission district, *Latinoamerica* depicted subject matter from Venezuela, Bolivia, Mexico, and Peru. The mural narrative created a vision of a native harmony with nature, using symbolic plants, animals, and ceremonies.

Often regarded by male muralists as apolitical, the Mujeres Muralistas rather chose to underscore indigenismo with work that created positive images of healing, danzas, elders, and nature. One mural, *Para El Mercado*, continued the portrayal of community and family through the narrative of harvesting and fishing in a rural setting. This depiction of women engaged in community labor cast women as primary participants in material production for their families.

While the Mujeres Muralistas were contributing murals to the community, they were strengthening their own indigenous traditions; Patricia Rodriguez, Irene Perez, and Mujeres Muralistas assistant Ester Hernandez were committed to Indigena organizing. As artists they contributed their work to such publications as *Indigena*, developed out of student efforts at the University of California at Berkeley during the mid-1970s. Issues of importance for Indigenas centered on what we would now call environmental racism. Early concerns about uranium dumping in the Native communities of the Southwest, as well as the environment in Brazilian indigenous communities, preceded the now-fashionable cultural-eco movement. Many Xicanas joined pan-Indian benefits and networks. They traced their family histories and genealogies, which often connected them with Pueblo, Apache, and Yaqui ancestry in the Southwest. It is important to note that once again the creation of indigenous images was not simply a visual mythology, but in many cases an active part of day-to-day history and political action. Beyond the brief period of their collective activities, the Mujeres Muralistas carried on the tradition of indigenous imagery through their individual mural work and served as an inspiration to other women artists and groups.

The legacy of Indigenas includes the work of artistas-Toltecas such as Carmen Lomas Garza, whose ongoing pictorial narratives of curanderismo, indigenous healing practices, have affirmed the powerful spiritual traditions of the Southwest. Linda Vallejo, a descendant of old California ancestry, has dedicated her artistic production to ritual ceremonias, with visual and dance components, while artists like Yreina Cervantes have produced watercolors and murals linking the indigenous roles of Central American and Chicana figures. A striking characteristic of the development of indigenous identity for many of these women has been the role of their grandmothers, *las abuelas*. The abuelas remain potent cultural sanctuaries for oral traditions of Indian heritage, spiritual practices such as home altars, and daily histories as Indian women. Artists like Judith Francisca Baca credit their female lineage and the critical influence of their grandmothers in redeeming a lost indigenismo.

Xicana artists made consistent use of images of Meso-American female deities, including Coatlique, the mother goddess, and Coyolxuahlqui, the moon goddess, in affirming their ancient ancestry. But perhaps the most important phenomenon of the indigenous for women was the integral relationship of art to social practice in both their artistic production and their community organizing.

In selecting these three grupos, other collectives cannot be overlooked. Groups such as the Royal Chicano Air Force (RCAF) of Sacramento, led by Jose Montoya, made valuable contributions to the history of indigenous practices among Xicanos through the Fieta de Maiz, the use of sweathouses for spiritual purification, and involvement with the Rio Grande Institute of New Mexico.

The grupos and Toltecas described above were participants in consolidating an indigenous Xicano identity in their regions and through national efforts. Each group and leader produced new aesthetic forms, language, and contemporary concepts affirming Amerindian beliefs in a popular barrio context. From Alurista's Annual Festival Flor y Canto (now Kanto del Pueblo) to Teatro's annual Virgen de Tepeyac, and Mujeres Muralistas' public works, traditions of a uniquely Xicano indigenismo have been established. The fusing of militant activism, popular practices, new Mexicano traditions, and native scholarship has brought indigenismo into the current setting of Xicano political thought and action.

But first el CHICANO must mexicanize himself
para no caer en cultural trampas
and that means that
not Thomas Jefferson or Karl Marx
will LIBERATE the Chicano
not Mahatma Ghandi or Mao Tze Tung
IF HE IS NOT LIBERATED FIRST BY HIS
PROPIO PUEBLO.

BY HIS POPOL VUE
HIS CHILIM BALAM
HIS CHICHEN ITZA
KUKULCAN, GUCUMATZ, QUETZALCOATL
y que lindo es estudiar
lo de su pueblo de uno
we must become NEO-MAYAS
porque los Mayas
really had it together

                                            — *Luis Valdez*

III. MEMORIA/FUTURO

In the course of examining *Palabras* (language), which conceptualized the indigenous, the issue of naming arose. A critical sense of origin, self-representation, and self-determination is realized in the naming process. Not only does naming identify the self, it marks a place. Circumscribing space, or defining the boundaries of place, is the marking of a geopolitical reality for the Xicano. Denoting where we stand and what we stand for is part of the marking of the boundaries of barrio, region, nationhood, and even cultural borders—knowing what we are by what we are not. The affirmation of family and working-class values continues in the face of exploitation and racism. The numbers of those of our community living under continuously perilous conditions continues to grow. In these communities, where single immigrant women are predominantly the sole heads of households, we are reminded of the original motivations for the development of collective actions in support of the people. And as we reflect on the resistance and contestation characteristic of the early movement over twenty years ago, it is alarmingly appropriate to current concerns.

As Deluvina Hernandez stated in 1970:

> The movement is a concept that is many things to many people, but to all it is the perpetuation of cultural and ethnic identity, and the betterment of social, economic and political conditions for Mexican people in the United States. The movement is practical in the sense that it aims to correct or abolish actual and perceived cultural, social, economic and political injustices and unwarranted hostilities towards the Mexican American collectively in the United States. It aims to liberate the group from social bondage to the dominating groups and classes of this country.[9]

The work of the three California-based groups presented in this paper reflect three major regional as well as cultural positions. The contributions of Alurista, Luis Valdez, and the Mujeres Muralistas in establishing guiding indigenous principles in a contemporary age are inestimable. Indigenous philosophy influenced their aesthetic forms, the collective nature of the grupos, the thematic content of their art, the practices of community engagement, and most of all, the passionate intention of their work.

Having established this foundational period, its themes, beliefs, and leadership, we face the greater question of its current meaning. In the neocolonial, post-Civil Rights era we see a major increase in Latino immigration, the introduction of more restrictive immigration policies, the potential displacement of Mexican Indians with the implementation of the Free Trade Agreement, and the rise of the Third World within First-World borders. Throughout this period of immigration we have witnessed the push of U.S. interventions in Latin America and with them the rise of death squads, *desaparecidos* ("the disappeared"), and practices of genocide—particularly of indigenous people—in El Salvador, Guatemala, Bolivia, and Peru.

Awareness of notions of a global village is an outgrowth of an ever-powerful media that depicts the cultures of the world, especially Latinos, as homogeneous. The so-called Latin Boom has been guided by marketing strategies. Racism in the United States is on the rise, and even terms like *people of color* cannot encompass the complex identites that include race, color, class, nationality, citizenship, language, gender, and sexual preference. Even the loss of natural resources through Native genocide in the Amazon draws the consciousness to a new period of *nueva-colonialismo*, or neocolonialism.

Xicanos must critically reaffirm and exercise their consciousness as indigenous communities when facing this crisis of survival. The recent marking of time in the 500-year span of foreign intervention in the New World has challenged the Xicano community to reflect on the absorption of Native peoples from Mexico and Central America. What new aspects of the indigenous core communities will affect the ongoing identity of American-born Xicanos?

Looking toward our Native brothers and sisters of North America we see their unrelenting efforts to return the remains of their ancestors to their rightful resting places, and we are reminded of the tens of millions of Meso-Americans whose lives were lost in the first century of Spanish invasion. Despite the hybrid and multilayered histories of conquests and mestizajes, the base of Xicano ancestry remains largely indigenous.

The refashioning of our early emphasis on indigenous self-representation is at the center of a contemporary response to new economic and social issues; it is conscious practice of self-preservation. It has been the discontinuous, fragmented, and dynamic interpretations of indigenismo that have become more real than the false institutional history of the Americas.

As we are drawn back to Alurista's indigenismo we see the interpretation of two currents—the validation of indigenous values and a critical evaluation of the modern role of the Indian. This integration of double currents is at the heart of a new sensibility and understanding of Xicano identity and political action.

Unlike the first Xicano age of indigenismo, which was largely dominated by male figures, the new indigenismo is reflected in the continuing work of women Toltecas, whose cultural narrative speaks of mothers, children, the elderly, and the poor. In this new age of colonialism in the Americas, we often see Latin women leading the resistance. Mothers of los desaparecidos, labor unionists, teachers, and farmworkers are at the forefront. Farmworker Dolores Huerta and human rights advocate Rigoberta Menchu are some of the individuals who come to mind.

Artists such as the Xicana-Yaqui Ester Hernandez, previously with the Mujeres Muralistas, have continued the depiction of images of defiance in contemporary works such as *The Weaving of the Disappeared*. Raised in a strongly matriarchal family with high-spirited women, and artistically directed in women's collectives, Hernandez expands images of the Native woman. Through narrative portraiture she has created a contemporary iconography of the female, including *ancianas*, or elders, women with children, historic figures, *antepasadas* (ancestors), and artistas. Working with other indigenous women, she is part of a growing network linking Amerindians across the United States. Legendary artist Judy Baca continues her work in mural collectives and in her Great Wall Mural Project in Los Angeles, which have called attention to indigenous and Third World issues. Her current work on the international portable mural structures of the World Wall will link Xicanos with Indian cultures and artists in Mexico.

The conferences and gatherings of Native women are increasing across the Southwest as traditional approaches are applied to new social conditions. The significance of alliances, collectives, and inter-American efforts is significant in this time of cultural emergency. Within such alliances this historic commitment to indigenismo must be recalled in a unity of purpose if our cultural lives on this continent are to continue. Thus, retrospection and introspection allow us once again to redefine this philosophy of our ancestral link.

Ultimately the Xicano nation has come to look upon the early years of the Xicano Movement as a time of great philosophic and ideological meaning in the advancement of our group life. (Re)thinking and (re)calling ourselves are part of our struggle. The internalized consolidation of our indigenous identity requires a time of reflection, so that the spirit of Amerindia may be once again for us a timeless symbol of opposition to cultural imperialism. The same strategic and operational devices of self representation, cultural revitalization, and pan-Indian collaborations are lessons in this new age of cultural emergency. The end of the millennium and the needs of the pueblo drive us to resourcefully restate our indigenismo in broad-based acts of unity.

ENDNOTES

1. J. Jorge Klor de Alva, "California Chicano Literature and Pre-Columbian Motifs: Foil and Fetish" (paper), p.19.
2. Tomas Ybarra-Frausto, "Alurista's Poeticas: The Oral, the Bilingual, the Pre-Columbian," in Joseph Sommers and Tomas Ybarra-Frausto, eds., *Modern Chicano Writers* (Englewood Cliffs, N.J.: Prentice-Hall, 1979), pp.120-21.
3. Chon Noriega, *In Aztlan: The Films of the Chicano Movement, 1969-79,* Whitney Museum of American Art 56, New Americas Film and Video Series (1991).
4. "El Plan Espiritual de Aztlan," manifesto, First Chicano Youth Liberation Conference at the Crusade for Justice (Denver, 1969).
5. Tomas Ybarra-Frausto and Shifra M. Goldman, *Arte Chicano: A Comprehensive Annotated Bibliography of Chicano Art, 1965-1985,* Chicano Studies Publication Unit, University of California (Berkeley, 1985), p.38.
6. Somers and Ybarra-Frausto, *Modern Chicano Writers,* p.124.
7. Guillermo Gomez-Pena, "A New Artistic Continent," in *Made in Aztlan,* Central Cultural de la Raza 15th Anniversary Exhibition Catalogue (San Diego, 1986).
8. Luis Valdez, *El Teatro Campesino: The First 20 Years, Birds and Serpents,* Anniversary Catalogue (San Juan Bautista, Calif.,1965).
9. Tomas Ybarra-Frausto, "Califas," conference proceedings, University of California (Santa Cruz).

PART II
BATTLE STANCES

"BATTLE STANCING"

TO DO CULTURAL WORK IN AMERICA

Bernice Johnson Reagon

As professionals who work in culture, we sometimes see a major difference between working with the various materials of our specific cultural legacies and carrying out the battles necessary to make this work a dynamic part of the larger cultural base within our society.

Why can't we just get on with our work? If we are to do public programs, why can't we just do great public programs? If we are to do exhibits, why can't we do exhibits? Why do we also have to be engaged in major military strategies and tactics for survival? These are sentiments I hear expressed all the time by many of my colleagues working in the area of community-based culture in our local communities or within regional or national forums. We all feel and often express real frustration at the energy and resources we have to marshall in order to create, expand, *and* protect territory in which to do our work.

We are African American, Asian American, Chicano; we are the Iroquois, the Hopi, the Puerto Rican Americans; we are women, we are the differently abled. We are all citizens of this land and a part of the cultural future of this society. Our constituencies are cultural and historical communities that have been neglected and attacked by a majority culture that upholds the principle of cul-

---

This essay is based on a presentation given at the Cultural Diversity Based on Cultural Grounding Conference in New York City in 1989.

tural dominance, which holds Western European culture and its derivatives as supreme.

We operate within a society that has made historic denial and distortion of our stories—and thus our existence—an integral part of the foundation upon which the country evolves. As specialists in the research and analysis, documentation, conservation, and dissemination of the cultural expressions of the communities we serve, we constantly struggle to keep some balance between doing the work of our professional training and engaging the challenges we must face so that we can do that work.

The establishment cultural and educational institutions that determine what is the core American experience, that determine what is and is not good or precious in the United States of America, know too little about us and do not want equitable representation of all cultures within the society. Those who determine the mission of these institutions often operate as if they do not know that ours is a nation of many peoples and many cultures. They dominate access to the resources that rightly belong to all whose labor and lives generated the resources.

Through our work as scholars, cultural programmers, art managers, community organizers, artists, educational specialists, or institution builders, some of us work to challenge monocultural dominance. We work in many ways so that we can bring an end to the false and crippling concepts of cultural dominance and superior knowledge. We see our work as a part of a contemporary struggle to bring into being a new national format, generated from a community base that will allow for the survival and prosperity of our cultural communities as equal partners within the society.

Most mainstream cultural institutions have developed programs in response to pressure to diversify the constituencies they serve. Efforts to expand cultural inclusion within these institutions often go wrong in regarding cultural systems that are outside of the dominant matrix as "other." While the rest of us are pushed to the periphery, occupying the restricted category of "other," the dominant cultural expressions are portrayed as being beyond culturally specific classification. The Eurocentric cultural legacy as it has evolved within the U.S. maintains its dominance by not identifying itself in such a specific way. Mainstream instititutions do their work, offering programs and conducting projects that are actually as culturally specific as anything I do that is African American. Western European derived expressions are presented, however, as if they are dictionary models—synonymous with what art, dance, theater, worship, education, music are. All else is specialized, is "other."

The systematic ways in which information and knowledge are ordered, and the control of access to the financial resources that support these networks operate as key instruments for perpetuating cultural inequity. Opening and transforming the information and knowledge base and sharing more equitably the funding pools is crucial to the natural growth and evolution of our various communities and the national community as a whole.

I myself came late to a consciousness of the way the dominant culture maintains its stance of superiority by controlling the ways in which knowledge is ordered and named and by controlling public resources intended for nurturing and disseminating cultural values to the society at large. Where I grew up, the school environment was the primary source of contact with this system of institutions. If there was a museum in my life, it was the living museum that is the community-based environment into which I was born. And it was certainly not called a museum or cultural center. Church, school, play, home, food, town, funerals—they all added up to a cultural network that balanced visions from the larger culture with those created by my people.

As I moved higher in the education system, the impact of organized and manipulated knowledge to perpetuate another system of cultural values increased. From the choirs in junior high and high school to the fine arts and lyceum series in college came news that there was a way to be; there was repertoire to recognize and appreciate if we were to get on in the world. The highest value was placed on bodies of knowledge outside of African American culture and history. Often African American existence was totally absent from the fountain of knowledge from which I and my fellow classmates had to drink. My parents and grandparents could not be my teachers in this new way of knowing, for it was not their way. I was blessed with African American teachers who cared about me as a person and about us as the collective new generation of African Americans. They taught me the lessons of the dominant culture, but they also taught me about Harriet Tubman, and they played games at recess that they could not have learned at college. My parents believed intensely in education and went through extraordinary means to ensure that their children had access to school. My mother was the primary agent in this effort, with my father acting as a strong partner. He had stronger connections with an older and more African-based system, in which people still believed in "working on people." They both, like many African Americans, believed that people have souls, and we all participated in sacred community-based rituals evolved for the nurturance and development of souls as real as flesh. My teachers and my parents believed that we had to become proficient in the ways of the dominant culture, while also maintaining a proficiency with the culture we were born into—the one not taught in schoolbooks.

I believed and excelled and for a time consumed all that was offered. Then came the 1960s and with them many new experiences: being thrown in jail for marching through the streets of my hometown; or going to the local library with a group of African American students, only to have the head librarian close the doors to all, rather than let us enter. Then came my suspension from college—a result of being jailed for demonstrating in support of fellow students, who themselves had been arrested for violating segregation laws (then already declared illegal) at the local Trailways bus station.

In jail we sang when we could not talk together, because we were old and young, poor and middle class, students and ministers' wives, street and church, tired and hungry, and dirty and too crowded. In jail we sang, and in jail I found out that some of the music I'd learned in music appreciation and voice classes and had sung in my choir repertoire—including the German lieder, Italian arias, and the big anthems—were of no use in comforting the spirit or in bonding a group of sixty-plus women crammed into the Lee County Stockade.

But there was a body of music that we all knew and shared that served us well during those times. The songs came from within our local community—from the church, the street, the talent show, the football game, from the top forty, and the teachers who had taught us spirituals they had been taught by their parents and teachers. The songs came old, as we had learned them generation after generation, and they came new—from radical students who were organizing anybody willing to risk their lives and future to confront and destroy racism.

I lived through the reality that my school and many of its administrators would not fight for change. I lived through the fight that those of us students, teachers, businessmen and women, church and street people waged. This was a struggle that demanded we stop everything—school and home—and give full attention and commitment to the fight for freedom. And we gladly and angrily paid the price. We had a chant then that went:

I don't want no mess
I don't want no jive
I want my freedom
by sixty-five.

It sort of expressed the quick-fix sense that the work of fighting racism was temporary and ephemeral. Fighting racism kept us from our real work. It was a phenomenon we had to deal with for a time — meet the challenges and opportunities and then, victorious, go on with the rest of our lives. As Movement workers, we stopped our everyday rhythms—left schools, jobs, homes—joined the fight; we were going to whip segregation and then get back to the real work we were made to do. Real work could be anything—teacher, carpenter, preacher, secretary, doctor, plumber—any career-oriented work that people living within a free society could do. The work of the Movement was temporary, crisis oriented, something that stopped all other regular work. So often our participation in Movement work was of the put-my-life-on-hold-for-a-minute-while-I-fix-this-racism-nuisance variety.

This feeling that the Movement was temporary was ameliorated by another experience. For me, doing this work was where I first found personal and collective grounding—I found comfort, centering, I found my name. At a time when I was involved in activities that put my physical life at risk, I felt safer than at any other period. For the first time in my life, I knew and lived who I was—I knew where I wanted to be, and I could sing it through the old songs I had learned while growing up or by creating new ones. I could, with the air I breathed and the space I occupied with my body, express and hold territory in the name of freedom. I slowly became committed to a way to walk in the world, by which I would never be in a position where anyone but I would shape my vision of myself and the world I lived in.

As an African American and a scholar, I continue to root myself and my research and documentation of African American culture in the understanding that my people are central to the evolution of this nation. My specific concern is the world of cultural institutions within our society—the schools, theaters, museums, libraries, historical societies, art galleries, concert houses, and cultural centers. As this world in which I move and work has grown larger, I have come to understand how to keep that first taste of struggle in my life, and it has helped me to maintain consistency in anything I attempt to do. Although the issues change from civil rights to antiwar to Native American concerns, to Chicano labor struggles, to women's rights, to the safety of children, to the rights of homosexuals—the work I do must sound my name and echo the lives of the ancestors who gave me the songs and stories that I used when giving voice to those of us jailed in Albany, Georgia, in 1961.

I believe that my life work is ensuring that the sound of my voice and other voices like mine have access to the airwaves and other means of communication. For me, being alive means taking a stand throughout one's life, of holding to a system of values and ideas. One's particular job or training is only an instrument of that resolve.

My presence here today as a member of the professional staff of a major establishment is the result of that commitment to struggle and my decision to be a carrier of African American culture through all times that I happen to live and breathe in. In my work, I operate both within the culture of my people and through the cultural mediums of the larger society. More important, this work of being a specialist in the history of my people's culture is my way of being a participant in the ongoing battle waged in this society by its African American citizens. Vincent Harding, calling it "a river of struggle," writes of an unending effort to transform society so that we can be who we are in our own vision.

At first, as the river metaphor took life within me, I was unduly concerned about its apparent inexactness and ambiguity. Now, with the passing of time and the deepening of our vision, it is possible to recognize that we are indeed the river, and at the same time that the river is more than us—generations more, millions more. Through such an opening we may sense that the river of black struggle is people, but it is also the hope, the movement, the transformative power that humans create and that create them, us, and makes them, us, new persons. So we black people are the river; the river is us. The river is in us, created by us, flowing out of us, surrounding us, re-creating us and this entire nation. I refer to the American nation without hesitation, for the black river in the United States has always taken on more than blackness. The dynamics and justice of its movement have continually gathered others to itself, have persistently filled other men and women with the force of its vision, its indomitable hope. And at its best the river of our struggle has moved consistently toward the ocean of humankind's most courageous hopes for freedom and integrity, forever seeking what black people in South Carolina said they sought in 1865: "the right to develop our whole *being*."

Those of us who have become professionals within the establishment or heads of our local community arts organizations since the 1960's are a continuation of older struggles to transform this society. The battle has been for the liberation of the many cultures held captive in a system based on inequity and exploitation. We are all potentially part of the initiative to the create a more nurturing environment where cultural equity is the norm. The current positions we hold as cultural leaders/workers are the result of ongoing battles and are in turn instruments of that initiative.

If we are open to it, we can understand that the major reason we are where we are is that we are propelled by the historical ongoing struggle against racism. Our role then is one of continuity and creativity. We have to find new ways, in our times, from our various contemporaneous positions, to continue the quest for the society that celebrates all her children.

All of this can be stated in battle terminology. In guerrilla warfare, one often gets repositioned to hold new territory. The first thing you have to do is stabilize the territory so you can survive, and you do that by doing work. We too often err by calling this stabilization component real work—teaching, doctoring, building shelter, growing food—thus separating it from the political struggles we have to wage within our communities and within our institutions to hold, protect, and expand our positions.

We may be curators, cultural programmers, producers, artists; so we often think that if we are writing an exhibit script, we are doing what we were hired to do—real work. Yet if we are dealing with the issue of securing a budget commensurate with our institution's importance within the society—also a way of fighting racism—this is work that may get in the way of writing an exhibit script. And certainly, if we have to fight to maintain or even reclaim funding, we feel that things are out of order. If we have to take on our administrators to get our constituencies represented on policy levels, it feels like work that takes away resources from our "real" work. These other issues are of the category of things that we would like to see fixed and stay fixed. I hear so often, "We did this in the sixties!" We are enraged to find the same problem surface with each generation.

Sometimes those of us who find ourselves in leadership positions on new fronts within our society perceive that our positions are the result of individual victories won. We occasionally forget that in the U.S., African American professionals are not usually placed in positions of leadership if that can be avoided. The only way they get these positions is through organized, community-based struggles that put such pressure on the targeted institution that its only recourse is to provide new accessibility to minority professionals. These institutions change as little as possible, often seeking ways to respond to pressure for broader cultural representation without reordering their historical agenda and purpose.

Too often, once minority professionals are in an establishment institution, they forget why and how they were hired, and they begin to see the aims of their work as separate from what is needed by their constituency—or their chosen field of study. Their success within the establishment can then be misleading and is often misused to thwart efforts at furthering change.

Sometimes even the most progressive of us, who remember

that we are not in those positions because of our brilliance (some of us think we got those jobs because we are brilliant), but as a result of a struggle that has been waged in this country, still misread where we are. We think, for instance, that because I am at the Smithsonian heading a program in the cultural traditions of my people, the battle is over and the victory won. This is a mistake. We are still on a battleground, and we continue to be fired upon in new and inventive ways.

Personally, I had to come to a place where I understood that to serve the institution that employed me was to serve my base, the African American community. When, as a scholar, I maintain intellectual integrity about the story of the African American peoples within this and related lands, then I am doing the only job I was prepared to do. It did not matter that often the institution wanted something less and different. Mainstream establishment institutions operate out of a strategy that aims to bring in minority specialists without altering the basic power structure and without changing the myth of the American story. I had to come to terms with continuing my work when I knew doing so would create deep anxiety within the institution.

I use war metaphors because I believe that, as professionals, we can for our times be what Harriet Tubman was for hers in nineteenth-century America. I don't believe one can work in the areas in which we are working without many times feeling the fragility of our position. Sometimes we have to move forward thinking *This next step is going to get me killed or the work crippled or stopped.* Many times you will think you are going to die. I decided it would be very boring to be killed doing something somebody else wanted me to do. If you are going to wipe me out, make sure you wipe me out because I am doing what I have envisioned myself doing, no matter where I am in the universe. Some of our elders say that when you die, you are not done, they say that you can come back again. And some people say that when you get killed, you don't feel it no how. So you don't have to worry too much about people killing you. I experienced a new freedom when I came to understand that my base of operation was the territory between my taking on a position and my leaving it. The greatest protection I could give myself for survival was to work that territory as if it belonged to the constituencies and struggles that created the space.

One of the pressing issues facing locally based cultural organizations is the aggressive move being made by larger organizations to absorb funding that we have chiseled with our bare hands
out of the public tax base. These funds in local, state, and national programs are small and inadequate, but they were nonexistent
before the sixties. Our efforts shaped these funding initiatives; we
developed the mission of achieving cultural equity within our
communities and the guidelines by which to serve that agenda. It
is our money in the first place, and it is too little, but the struggle
for equity has nonetheless been carried on by professionals who
learned how to operate inside of the structure. So now, when the
decisionmakers in the art councils, the foundations, or the endowments get together, they at least *ask* the question, "What are we
going to do about minorities?" They wonder about ethnic representation. But they don't do this because they got up one morning
and discovered that we are a part of their society; they ask these
questions today because we forced this agenda.

No sooner had our efforts begun to result in funding for more
complex cultural constituencies than the mainstream institutions
themselves began to maneuver to take over the very resources we
had, through our lobbying efforts, created. Now when we send pro-
posals, we find ourselves in competition with them. Some of us
seem surprised that this would be their strategy. Some of us seem
surprised that we would have to fight to keep this territory we'd
won and to expand it. Once there were programs in place that
responded to community-based issues and to cultural expressions
from many cultures, the establishment institutions that dominated the funding structures—in order to underwrite the continuance
of symphony orchestras and Shakespeare theaters—turned to the
newly defined categories and competed with us to control the new
funding and the interpretation of the issue of multicultural diversity within the cultural arts community. Now they are requesting
funds from this same pot for underwriting their weak efforts to
diversify their offerings—leaving their central mission unchanged.

There are instances where the initial collaborations between
establishment institutions and community-based ones were based
on respect and acknowledgement, but in the second, third, or

fourth projects, the voice changes. The money still comes from the same place—the coffers earned in what Vincent Harding calls "the longest battle for freedom known in modern times." The community-based institutions, however, are no longer equal partners. The larger institutions have moved to establish control of the very subject matter they have so long ignored and distorted. In this way, many of our community-based efforts have been undermined.

It is important to stay in touch with the fact that the very agenda we have gathered to discuss at this conference, cultural equity, is an agenda we have created through our struggle. The country would not be talking about cultural diversity, outreach programs, minority expansion, cultural pluralism, multiculturalism, had our struggle not created the agenda. It is our efforts that have forced this nation to begin coming to terms with the cultural complexity of this society. We insisted upon it because it was the next step in a battle that has been going on since slavery.

The coopting of progressive initiatives has been one of the most significant responses the dominant society has made to agendas we've created. Name appropriation is key to this strategy of slowing down change. Terms born of community-based struggles are appropriated by mainstream society and redefined, so that multicultural diversity and multiethnic programs become another way of narrowing our access to resources. African Americans, for example, are made to compete with other ethnic communities, because we find ground that we have achieved renamed, so that the same territory must be shared by all who are now part of "the Other."

We respond to this strategy by creating new terms such as *cultural equity*, in hopes that this term will not also be used to create divisive confusion. We actually start having discussions and conferences that are no longer about power and resource sharing, but about terminology and decoding the naming process. If these sessions really sought to unveil the cooptation strategy for what it is and to outline ways to avoid the traps it sets, it would be beneficial. More often, though, these discussions inadvertently become instruments of the cooptation strategy, because our efforts are spent arguing about who means what when using a particular term.

Culturally specific programs and institutions should not be redefined as multicultural programs and institutions. The term *multiculturalism* should always identify efforts toward a coalition of many. It should always mean increased territory and resources for culturally specific groups as a whole. If there is a shift in balance, it should always come from the resource base that we have all been shut out of, that which is controlled by the cultural monopoly.

Most of us are not accustomed to find comfort in the sense that life and work are continuous struggles, or in the understanding that without motion one is almost always liable to lose ground. To the contrary, we have been trained to believe that success is related to fixing things so that they stay fixed by themselves; that a job well done is a job completed, which then allows one to move on to the really important work. Many of us are frustrated to find that in order to ensure the quality of the work, we have to build into any system constant monitoring and maintenance.

In the same way, many of us fail in personal relationships because we seem to expect that after an initial period of intense input, the bonding should hold indefinitely. When we find that things fall apart if they are not attended to consistently, we are annoyed or resentful. We have been socialized to expect that when we are confronted with a problem, we develop a plan of attack to take care of it, and that once that plan of action is executed, we can turn our attention to other things.

A personal example may make this clearer. I have a problem with food. I eat more than I need to eat to sustain my body. I have observed, incredulously, that some people use food only to stay alive, that they do not continue eating after they are full, they do not finish everything on their plates and go back for seconds or thirds. I have seen people actually take a bite of something, realize they don't like it or that they are not hungry, and put it down! Having become aware that overeating might not be the best way to take care of the business of living, I have mapped out and successfully executed multiple plans to bring my problem under control. Again and again, I have struggled to learn how to eat what I need to eat to keep my physical unit fueled and to leave the rest.

The truth is, I am furious to even have the problem. I am a good person, I lead a good life, why do I have this issue of my plate? What I really wanted to do was to give some intensive attention to the problem, execute a program or two, and then move on to some real work. I resent the fact that the minute I think I have my food problem under control and don't need to give it anymore time, I lose, or better stated, I gain. The truth is that for me I have to be constantly on my guard about what my plate looks like, and if I don't focus energy on that, then little else I want to do will be balanced. Somehow, the point of spending primary time on my body and its maintenance has escaped me. It seems to me to be a misuse of time that could be better spent in research, or writing, or singing, or organizing, yet I have to spend it on what my plate looks like, in order for me to stay under 200 pounds.

You may have other examples of wanting to take care of problems so that they stay taken care of forever. If you do, then you also have experienced the frustration of finding that the situation has escalated to a crisis level again and again. It did not stay fixed, as you had hoped, because you did not reorganize your life, energy, and resources to give it the constant monitoring and maintenance it required. We are often lulled by a false sense of calm and order if things seem to be progressing well. When we see the problem resurface, we assume that the last time we took care of it, we simply did not attend to it properly. If we had, it wouldn't be coming back, demanding to be addressed again.

These false assumptions cause us to be unprepared for what comes up on our agenda. One cannot breathe once and expect that the task of getting oxygen is completed. Every breath of air that goes into your lungs has to be pulled in. When you paint a wall you cannot do ten strokes and then expect the wall to cover itself. Every area that needs to be painted has to be gone over with brush or roller. The natural order of things in the universe indicates that life itself is not a ditto affair. I do not know of any living thing that can be changed and challenged—transformed—and remain so without major effort and energy.

I am making a case for the continuity of stancing, so that you understand that as long as you are alive, some of your energies have to be given to the stance and the values of that stance. Time and energy have to be given to managing, securing, and advancing your territory as a vital and integral part of the real work you do. If you, in your living and your work, do not invest energy in the things you care about all the time, you will find yourself with less space to operate in to express your concepts.

We can all be a part of the battle to expand enough territory so that our peoples—laden with our histories, our traditions, and our rituals—can be ushered through this tenuous time. As it is struggle, it is also dance, celebration—we live and work toward a promise of a fuller life. It is a very normal position to be in, if we remember that we have arrived at this place where we talk about cultural equity and the survival of our cultural communities and thus our peoples, as an integral part of a historical process. No matter what our work, what our training, what our status, we are also the frontline of the continuing struggle to make this society a place where we can be who we are.

REFERENCE

Harding, Vincent. *There Is a River: The Black Struggle for Freedom in America*. New York: Harcourt Brace, 1981.

CULTURAL DIVERSITY

AN ASIAN AMERICAN PERSPECTIVE

Margo Machida

Underlying the question posed to this panel, "Are Western European culturally specific institutions obsolete?" is a fundamental belief we share that the predominance of Eurocentric values and practices in American culture must be challenged and new institutional models and cultural policies be put forward that are respectful and supportive of the heritages of *all* Americans. Such a belief is rooted in the urgency and outrage we feel at seeing our communities historically underserved, disregarded, and disenfranchised, and their growth stunted by political interests and legislation reflecting a strongly Eurocentric bias (as with the discriminatory immigration laws that long had limited Asians' entry into the United States). In the realm of cultural politics, where we must compete for dwindling public funding with relatively well-supported "Western European culturally specific institutions" reflective of the interests of such dominant groups, a major thrust has been to aggressively and publicly criticize those institutions as embodying, serving, and perpetuating the very power structures and belief systems that devalue our communities and the art that emanates from them. Thus, we engage in "turnabout" politics: literally, to turn the tables and declare *Eurocentric* institutions obsolete, parochial, and culturally irrelevant given the

---

These remarks were delivered at the Cultural Diversity Based on Cultural Grounding II Conference in New York City on October 18, 1991.

changing demographics of this society, and, implicitly, to replace them with our own images and visions of American culture.

What I'd like to suggest is that such confrontational positions alone—while politically effective (and certainly all of us have used them)—can also be limiting, if they are not considered as part of a broader range of approaches for advocacy, since they do not allow for a more complex reading of the problems presently confronting our diverse institutions. In other words, in this rapidly changing American cultural scene, we must attempt to get beyond the limitations inherent in the politics of anger, the seemingly unbridgeable us-them dichotomy—in order to develop more subtle and complex strategies for the future.

SCENARIOS FROM THE ASIAN AMERICAN VISUAL ARTS FIELD

I'd like to briefly sketch out three scenarios from the Asian American visual arts arena that typify some of the problems our communities face in dealing with the American arts environment—which I believe also have relevance for other ethnic and racial groups.

Right now, the Asian American visual arts "scene" is quickly being transformed. In addition to the community arts organizations that have been the Asian American cultural movement's bedrock since the 1970s, there are more diverse "players" than ever before. They represent different Asian nationalities, generations, economic groups, and political orientations. Grassroots cultural organizations serving the most recent Asian immigrants are springing up daily. New institutions specific to the more established Asian American nationality groups, like the Japanese American National Museum in Los Angeles, have also been founded. We're witnessing the emergence of a highly diverse field—a historic moment of great potential, requiring an ever broader array of arts institutions to support these cultural developments.

Meanwhile, outside these communities, there are parallel trends that are also impacting on our field. As I'll later elaborate, with the emphasis on multiculturalism and funding incentives for audience development, large-scale museums and comparable institutions are beginning to reach out to Asian Americans—primarily through educational and public programming. How will we relate to these efforts? Further, there have been some high visibility exhibitions developed jointly by American and Asian cultural institutions, which to some suggests the possibility of new Asian funding sources for Asian Americans. In this increasingly complex situation, the major problem confronting Asian American artists, administrators, and cultural organizations is to decide how to position ourselves in relation to this widening field of possibilities—to insure that our communities receive meaningful and continuing attention.

Let's consider *Scene A. GODZILLA Goes to the Whitney Museum of American Art.* The recent dealings between GODZILLA: Asian American Art Network and the Whitney raise significant questions about how Asians and other communities of color can address our continuing exclusion from the so-called mainstream arts institutions that claim to be inclusive of artists and work reflecting a broad range of issues and communities constituting contemporary American culture.

In brief, following the 1991 Whitney Biennial—a major group exhibition presenting a spectrum of contemporary art from across the nation deemed significant—GODZILLA noted that *no* Asian American visual artists were featured in the painting, sculpture, and photography section. This reflected a longstanding pattern of noninclusivity. Accordingly, GODZILLA wrote a letter of protest to David Ross, the Whitney's recently appointed director, underscoring the problem and offering to meet with him and his staff to discuss what might be done to correct this situation. The letter was intentionally given wide distribution to other museums, funding agencies, and art publications—to raise public awareness of issues concerning Asian American artists. Five months later, Mr. Ross requested a meeting with group representatives, which took place in September, 1991. While identifying long-term goals such as the inclusion of Asian Americans in exhibitions and the permanent collection, and as staff, consultants and members of the board, GODZILLA also advocated for short-term projects, such as curatorial visits to Asian American artists' studios, facilitated by the group; and the establishment of an annual multiracial curatorial roundtable, sponsored by the Whitney, at which scholars and curators could share information on work and issues emanating from diverse communities. Throughout, our aim was to promote the creation of ongoing, institutionalized mechanisms for dialogue between our communities and the museum. To date, Mr. Ross has agreed to allow GODZILLA to submit twelve artists' slides to his curators, to review for possible visits; other possibilities are under discussion, however. [*Author's note*: Since this writing, some artists recommended by GODZILLA, all intentionally selected from outside the organization's membership to prevent conflicts of interest, have been contacted for studio visits by Whitney curators.]

Then there's *Scene B. Against Nature: Japanese Art in the Eighties.* This traveling exhibition, featuring ten contemporary Japanese artists and artist groups, exemplifies the growing presence of high visibility exhibitions showcasing contemporary Asian art—meaning art produced by Asian artists in Asia, rather than by Asian Americans. It was co-organized by the Grey Art Gallery at New York University, the Massachusetts Institute of Technology List Visual Arts Center, and the Japan Foundation, and it has toured widely throughout the United States for the past two years. This ambitious project involved both American and Japanese curators and received substantial support from the Japan Foundation, the National Endowment for the Arts, the Asian Cultural Council, and the Bank of Boston, among others. The emergence of such crosscultural initiatives seems to signal that deep pockets of Asian funding exist, which are ripe for tapping by Asian Americans. In fact, this interest in things Asian often does not extend to Asian American artists and institutions; the presence of Asian or Asian-directed corporate and foundation support does not automatically translate into money for our indigenous institutions and communities.

As Asian and other foreign corporations make commitments to staying in America, however, they are gradually developing policies for corporate giving. A long-term strategy must be developed for sensitization and education of such potential supporters to the range of communities comprising American society—if the smaller community organizations are to benefit from their funding at all. Too often, however, the big museums and the most spectacular national projects absorb their attention, because they are maximal opportunities for good public relations. To put it crudely, the foreign corporations want the biggest "bang for the buck." Educating such entities about social responsibility and the importance of the arts as vital expressions for the lives of all communities is a goal worth considering. Again, the position paper—in combination with other strategies— may be a tool in initiating this process.

Scene C is a more generalized and increasingly prevalent scenario, whereby large-scale museums and comparable cultural institutions are beginning to do outreach to Asian American artists and communities. This has resulted from a combination of factors: the rise of multiculturalism as a national issue; funding agency guidelines that require institutions to demonstrate their efforts to include diverse artists and audiences; and special monies being set aside for audience development initiatives. The last issue—as you know—has sparked bitter debates about how public monies should be spent, whether for outreach efforts by large, comparatively well-funded institutions that have a history of making little more than sporadic or token efforts, or for the community organizations that directly serve their populations. How will we relate to this situation? Do we recommend that all funding for outreach be discontinued, resulting in the perpetuation of the status quo? Conversely, who determines what a "fair" percentage of funding for such initiatives should be?

STRATEGIES FOR CHANGE

In dealing with situations such as those I have just outlined, the primary question is how we, as members of diverse communities, can make our needs manifest. The hard truth is that Eurocentric institutions will not disappear; so long as they serve the interests of a broad segment of the American population, they will continue to exist as part of the landscape and to receive support. We then have several different options: to oppose their existence and validity as representative of American culture; to take a separatist position and develop our own culturally rooted parallel institutions; and/or to devise collaborative, dialogic strategies and policies to insure that our communities can participate in, help to shape, and benefit from the services these larger institutions are funded to provide. What I'm suggesting is that rather than an either/or approach, we need to allow for a complex landscape in which *many* strategies receive our support and cooperation.

For example, the scene with GODZILLA and the Whitney raises many strategic issues about how Asian Americans (or any other group) can have an ongoing impact—both at the policy and programmatic level—on existing Eurocentric institutions that have historically excluded or ignored them. The first step was indeed confrontational—to get our issues heard by making very public the museum's obvious exclusion of Asian American visual artists in the last Biennial. Yet, without financial leverage, which is the bottom line for most institutions, ultimately the only authority of outside interest groups is moral: urging such institutions to recognize that to "live up" to their claims of being truly inclusive, they must involve all groups comprising American society—and see as meaningful the issues that arise from those artistic communities. In such an instance, a policy paper developed by this body might be extremely useful in providing philosophical guidelines for consideration by these large Eurocentric institutions.

In closing, I'd like to urge that we examine current models for cooperative strategies among our various arts communities-including the Western European-oriented institutions—that create contexts for us to meet on a coequal footing. We can regard exhibitions like "The Decade Show: Frameworks of Identity in the 1980s," co-organized in 1990 by the Museum of Contemporary Hispanic Art, The New Museum of Contemporary Art, and The Studio Museum in Harlem, as experiments in intracommunity collaboration—an undertaking that was certainly problematic in many respects, but still represented an important initiative that has resulted in relationships that are still ongoing. Such projects do not diminish us, but rather they expand the range of possibilities that point toward a future in which the multivalent nature of American art and culture will be commonly accepted and supported.

AMERICAN INDIANS, EUROPEAN CONTACT, AND THE DOCTRINE OF DISCOVERY

Gawanahs, Tonya Gonnella Frichner
(Onondaga Nation)

*Where are the Pequot? Where are the Narragansett, the Mohican
and many other once powerful tribes of our people? They have
vanished before the avarice and the oppression of the white man,
as snow before a Summer Sun.*

—Tecumseh (Shawnee)

Sigolli, Greetings, from the territory of the Haudenosaunee,
Six Nations Iroquois Confederacy. Our territories traditionally ran
from what is present-day northern Quebec and Ontario to the
Carolinas and as far west as the tributaries of the Ohio River. The
Haudenosaunee, our traditional name for ourselves, maintain the
oldest continuing democracy in the world and continue to exercise
our rights as a sovereign nation. Onondaga, the nation from which
I come, is located in northern New York State. The city of Syracuse
sits on our territory, and it pays us rent for that privilege. The peo-

This presentation was part of the panel "From the Dominance of the Few to
the Liberation of the Many: New Definitions" at the Cultural Diversity Based
on Cultural Grounding II Conference in New York City on October 17, 1991.

ple of the Six Nations also travel on passports issued by our government.

It is estimated that in 1492 Indians in the Western Hemisphere constituted between 72 million and 112 million people. Where did they all go? What happened to them?

In 1552, the Spanish Catholic priest Bartolome de las Casas, conducting the first census in the Americas, declared that in the fifty years since the Spanish invasion, 50 million Indians had perished. Las Casas had been an eyewitness to some of the slaughter and had protested these cruelties. He asserted that 5 million Indians had died in the Caribbean Islands and that 45 million had died on the mainland. Debate over the exact numbers continues, but diverts attention away from the main issue: the theft of the Western Hemisphere by unjust and atrocious means. The inability of Native labor to support the colonists' industries because of their rapid decline in number led directly to the import and enslavement of peoples from Africa.

From the landing of the first European on these shores until comparatively recently, the history of the United States has been influenced by its Indian inhabitants to a degree far out of proportion to our numbers. The dominant culture can never forget that we were here first and that we are entitled to survival rather than extinction. Yet this history is not supported by accurate knowledge; it is supported by stereotypes. We do not and did not all live in tepees, wear the war bonnets of Plains cultures, or even share the same language. Our Nations are as many and as diverse as the European nations that arrived on our shores.

Five hundred years ago Christopher Columbus arrived in the Western Hemisphere. He did not, however, discover the "New World"—our world. Ours was an ancient world, with our own history, culture, traditions, commerce, technologies, sciences, and systems of government. Principles of democracy, such as freedom of speech, freedom of religion, individual rights, the rights of women to participate in government, the concepts of separation of powers in government, and of checks and balances of power within government were in place for many centuries. These principles were all part of the constitution of my people, called the Great Law of Peace. Many centuries ago, a man called the Peacemaker, brought the Great Law of Peace to the warring factions of the Five Nations. Through his efforts, the peoples of the Longhouse, the Haudenosaunee, were brought together under one supreme law governing the Confederacy of the Onondaga, Mohawk, Cayuga, Oneida, and Seneca.

For us the arrival of Columbus marked the beginning of a long holocaust—a genocide as deliberate and merciless as Hitler's murder of the Jews. We were consumed by the fevers of newly encountered diseases, the flashes of settlers' and soldiers' guns, the ravages of firewater, and the flames of villages and fields burned by the scorched-earth policy of vengeful Euro-Americans. Unlike the Jews, many Indian Nations became extinct. Between 1492 and the present day, the population of each of the European nations increased between five and ten times. Today, even with the twentieth-century gains in population, Native survival is less than 50 percent of 1492 levels.

This tradition of war and conquest was latent in the civilization of Europe, an aspect of its Christian heritage. The early Christian message spoke for the weak and oppressed. Its message was one of peace and nonviolence, one our ancestors would have understood. But by the time Christianity arrived on our shores, it had hardened in a mold of bigotry, intolerance, militancy, and greed, making it our enemy. The teachings of Christ were reinterpreted into rules of conduct for nation states. War and violence were redefined in Christian terms. The theory of "just" war became one that could be used for economic and social expansion across the Americas, later called Manifest Destiny. To the Christian state, being "your brother's keeper" justified intervening in international affairs and elevated the imposition of the European political system to a moral obligation.

Columbus, the "Christ Bearer," as his name and mission implied, seemed to bring closer the day when all the world would be Christian. This arrogant spirit is echoed in the famous Bull Inter Caetera of May 3, 1493, which the Spanish rulers obtained from the Pope upon Columbus's return. The bull conveyed the Pope's expectation that Spain convert the Indians, a responsibility the Spanish interpreted as permitting every injustice in the name of conversion. The status of Indians was defined by Catholic doctrine and Spanish law from the moment of contact. Indians were condemned as a material resource to be exploited and as spiritual objects to be saved. Out of that dehumanization was born the mentality of racism. In 1550 the Spanish Crown called for a debate to be held before the Council of the Indies in Valladolid to determine whether Indians were true human beings. Dr. Juan Gines de Sepulveda, sometimes referred to as the father of modern racism, argued before the council that the conquistadors had a right to treat Indians as beasts. It was also necessary to convince the Spanish people that Indians were not only inferior, but that they were barbarians incapable of producing thinkers and philosophies that could be helpful to European settlers.

The history of contact brings us to a discussion of American Indians and the origin of the sixteenth-century Law of Nations. The Law of Nations developed as a process through which European nations could legally expropriate or steal the land in this hemisphere from its original inhabitants. The expansion of one people into the territory of another has rarely involved the application of legal or moral theories to safeguard the rights of the original inhabitants. The Law of Nations, also known as the Doctrine of Discovery, was a theory of the right of exploitation. The absence of rights to dignity and culture, land, and ultimately existence, remains one of the central legacies of the Doctrine of Discovery. According to the United Nations, today there are about 170 nation states that claim dominion over 3,000 to 5,000 indigenous cultures.

The Doctrine of Discovery, an agreement among the European states competing for territory, ensured that the state that arrived first at a place would have first rights to explore and colonize that place. This "right of discovery" was later applied to lands whether or not they were occupied by people. In fact, under such principles the existence of distinct peoples became legally irrelevant. This agreement developed principally because it was more expedient for individual nations to compromise their claims than to fight over them. States simply drew lines of demarcation and established territories based on them. Besides being expedient, this was considered good business.

Initially, Indian Nations had relations with many European governments. When the Doctrine of Discovery came into play, however, Indian Nations could deal only with the European nation selected to steal its territory. All others were bound by the doctrine to stay away. As a result, Indian nations were excluded from the international community, an arena in which many of them had played a very active role. For example, initially the Haudenosaunee had relations and treaties with the Dutch, French, and British.

During the era of colonization in America, the European countries did, however, mutually agree that any curtailment of the sovereign powers of Indian tribes should be done only by the consent of the Indians themselves. The framers of the U.S. Constitution recognized this international commitment when they acknowledged that treaties were the "supreme law of the land." But the U.S. government began to deal with Indian Nations as if they were part of the U.S. population and not as distinct nations outside the purview of the government. Over the past 200 years, the international policy of consent has lost its meaning entirely.

Today, Indian Nations are subject to the plenary control of Congress and the courts, a power that is complete, absolute, and unqualified. Because there is no constitutional basis, the plenary doctrine was created by the United States Supreme Court. It developed from what the Court viewed as a void in congressional powers over Indian tribes.

Although I do not speak for all Indigenous people, I will attempt to answer the question, What do Indigenous people want?

We want recognition of our distinctiveness. The right to keep our territory and to regain land that was illegally expropriated, so that we may have a land base adequate to support our people. In other words, we want the right to a physical existence and the right to preserve a separate identity—including culture, language, and social and legal institutions that are respected and recognized by the community of nations. Assimilation, on the other hand, is the ally of extermination. Insistence on assimilation undercuts the recognition of the distinct nature and rights of Indians as Indians.

While the gun, the Bible, the dollar, and the bottle did destroy many of us, we are still here as a people. Our story is not over.

Da nay to [I am finished].

A VISION FOR BLACK COMMUNITY RECONSTRUCTION

David Bryan

Like many of you, I am here in multiple roles, as an independent arts consultant, as an arts producer, and as an active citizen. I became involved in the arts through an interest in, or more precisely a political commitment to, Black advancement. As a consequence, I have been instrumental in developing several Black nonprofit and arts organizations in Britain. Therefore, I come to the arts as someone who wants to ensure that we have the managerial requirements for development. Talk of development may be difficult when mere survival is still the standard state of affairs, but the vision we hold must be one of a life beyond mere survival. Such a vision requires us to extend our thoughts into the political sphere, because culture, race, and politics are intimately related.

My experience with Brixton Village exemplifies that lesson. In 1989, when I left the post as its director, Brixton Village was the largest Black arts center in the country. Sadly, that institution is no longer operating in any capacity. Its decline highlights many of the issues raised here and is relevant to the title of this session, "After the Theoretical and Practical Framework Are in Place, What Next?: Towards an International Policy for Cultural Equity." I want

This talk was delivered at the Cultural Diversity Based on Cultural Grounding II Conference on October 18, 1991, in New York City. The subject of the panel was "After the Theoretical and Practical Framework Are in Place, What Next?: Towards An International Policy for Cultural Equity."

to share with you briefly the struggles that have led to the loss by the Black community, primarily in London, but also felt throughout the country, of an institution, a unique asset, a symbol of advancement.

Brixton is known not for its connections with world-famous artists such as David Bowie, and before him Charlie Chaplin, for whom Brixton was home for a significant period, or for its radical socialist council. Brixton is currently best known in Britain as the scene of two Black rebellions in the last ten years. Yet, while the media paint Brixton as a Black community, many of you here in the U.S. would be at a loss to understand the relevance of the racial label. Brixton has a declining (30 percent) Black population, mainly of Caribbean descent, mostly Jamaican, and Asians, Greeks, Italians, Africans, Latin Americans, and others. The richness of this cosmopolitan community, however, as is true of many of our experiences, is being highlighted as a beneficial feature only now, as the process of gentrification transforms Brixton.

When I was appointed to direct Brixton Village in 1984, it was a white Christian institution—to be precise, a dilapidated Anglican church, St. Matthew's—that was attempting to find new life by dabbling in community development. The church was, as were many other white churches in the inner cities, undergoing a crisis of purpose in the face of diminishing numbers, with many churches unable to muster more than a hundred parishioners. Acquisition of a government grant gave the church a new lease on life and the license to play missionary to the local natives, for now it had a new sense of purpose. The church acquired government funding on the basis of its important role as a facilitator of Black concerns. Those who had been excluded were now to be embraced. In 1980, before the first rebellion in Brixton, overt racism was commonplace, especially by the police. They made Black people targets of random stops-and-searches. It was acknowledged that they had instituted a color bar against Black people. Ironically, after the rebellions, Black people were faulted for not joining the police force. In Brixton itself, fewer than a dozen Black people could be found working in the area's main stores, banks, and so forth. In often released reports, government-funded agencies identified the existence of active racism at all levels of British society.

After employing a succession of white clergy-missionaries, St. Matthew's employed me as the first Black director of its church-cum-community center. Developing a potentially major institution in post-rebellion Brixton required that a vision for advancement and leadership be pursued. My vision was to establish an institution with a social, cultural, and religious dimension for the whole community. This vision was innovative, ambitious, and ahead of its time. With the institution now in Black hands, all sections of the community expected to have access to it. Applying the Anglican ecumenical approach, I expanded the Christian base to include those of other denominations, such as African and Pentecostal, and individual worshippers of non-Christian beliefs.

Within three years we had established ourselves as the cultural center for Black arts and community development. To reinforce this transformation we had changed the name from St. Matthew's Meeting Place to Brixton Village. The departure of St. Matthew's Meeting Place heralded the end of an era of white, Christian, liberals obstructing the progress of Black and ethnic minority peoples. Brixton Village affirmed in the local community mind, and later in the country's, that this was a Black-managed venture that was forward looking and nondiscriminatory. The birth of Brixton Village was cause for celebration in the Black community. It was an institution that would inspire and empower the community to fulfill their hopes and ambitions, with no boundaries. Since Brixton itself was viewed as Black, the new name served to more than locate the organization, it affirmed its Blackness. *Village* symbolized the village communities whence Black people originated.

The renaming and high profile sustained by Brixton Village offered us the opportunity to challenge the no-go-zone image of Brixton that the white media had created. Furthermore, given our unique blend of social, cultural, and religious activities, we provided a range of cultural experiences "from the cradle to the grave"—from christening ceremonies to funerals, with education, social welfare, and the arts in between. To achieve this vision, radical steps had to be taken, steps that were, at the time, outside the comprehension of the community. The Black staff team we inherited, who harbored notions and practices of mediocrity and dependency, had to be removed to make way for a new generation of Black workers who had the skills and determination to make a difference. (On my first journey to America, some 12 years ago, I was blessed to be at a Boston gathering at the home of activist Mel King, where we were addressed by a Black professor from Harvard, who had a great impact on me. We were advised to see ourselves as African village youths, energetic and bright hopefuls charged with going forth into the world to gain skills and experiences that we would later return to our villages for their benefit.) The efforts of this small team of miracle workers created the beacon of success that eventually opened the door to new realizations about the capabilities of Black people.

The financial base of Brixton Village came initially from the local council, which provided 80 percent of the center's income in the early years. In my last year, 1990, the local council's investment had declined in real terms to 20 percent of the total annual grant while our turnover had quadrupled from $120,000 to $525,000 in five years. The local council dramatically reduced its grant, and the London Arts Council gave a grant of $22,500, claiming that the center was "off the beaten track." At this time the center was generating nearly $300,000 and attracting funds from other sources on the basis of its success. The level of economic development and the degree of widespread local support and usage were not without their price.

Such success led us to lower our guard, since we were nearing the achievement of the target of self-financing. This success was not easily forged, but the existence of Brixton Village inspired many who once believed that Black people in Britain were incapable of doing anything in the cultural realm and beyond. Instead we affirmed the "I-am-somebody" concept, that indeed we can manage for ourselves. This important challenge to the eroding and undermining impact of racism was not without its enemies. The forces of destruction came from every quarter. Among the London arts community, Brixton Village was attacked as being too "popular" in approach, such as in our selection of arts events, and not concerned enough with cultural quality. The local council officials and politicians were embarrassed and challenged by our independent institution, which was leading a cultural and social regeneration in

Brixton when their own efforts and far greater resources were not achieving any results. Negotiations between St. Matthew's, which remained our landlord, and the local council took place in secret, with the agenda being the acquisition of Brixton Village by the council. (Just before I came to this conference I discovered that the local council were in negotiation with the church while I was attempting to establish Brixton Village's independence.) The Arts Council (equivalent to the National Endowment for the Arts) and its London body were unwilling to make funds available to us at a time when plans were in the pipeline for a large showpiece Black arts center. The Council seemed to fear that such a center would make the neighboring white institutions, which received funding of about $255,000 annually, look bad by comparison.

I had planned for Brixton Village to be economically independent and therefore beyond the influence of these opposing forces. Unfortunately, while we managed for two years without local council and Arts Council funding, we did not calculate that the collective forces of opposition would amass against Brixton Village. Despite this conspiracy, there was substantial support offered from the white business community and the charitable trust world, which clearly saw our vision as an answer to meaningful social and economic integration. Such was our success in attracting audiences that Brixton Village was given an award from the prominent London arts magazine, *Time Out,* for our innovative theater seasons. Until the existence of Brixton Village, it was thought by many in the arts that Black people did not attend the theater. Brixton Village revolutionized public perception in this area to the extent that Black theater is today still enjoying Black patronage.

In the end, the church sided with the local council in the struggle for control of Brixton Village. The Village as we knew it lasted less than two years after my departure in 1990 and that of the team that made our vision a reality. Now that the Village is closed, it is understood that the local council will reopen it and run it as its own venue.

I have shared this experience with you to illustrate that we can never, when building institutions, take support for granted or underestimate the threat that our success brings. The evidence of the last couple of days here at this conference is that where we have some degree of success, we must not become complacent. It is apparent that in the U.S. and in Britain social, political, and cultural gains are being eroded. In this respect, international alliances—on the level of exchanges of knowledge and experience— are clearly important. But I must express some caution, if not apprehension. We must be mindful of not slipping into imperial practices, even by default. Let me explain. Right now in Britain we are fed a regular diet of Black American films, such as *New Jack City, Boyz N the Hood, Juice,* and so on. The danger is obvious: Investment in the cultural experiences of Black people in Britain is not seen as important. Our cultural experiences continue to be unheard, unrecorded, and unvalued. America is seen as representing modernity, the future. Too much is made of the trite comment that what happens today in America will occur ten years later in Britain. This is far from the truth, yet we can see the impact of Black urban American culture on British youth, be they African, Caribbean, Asian, or white.

The mass media power brokers have "discovered" commercially viable Black products, which offer them the means to impose racist stereotypes of Black people around the world. Black communities, in Canada, England, or wherever, are finding that their own expressions are being driven into extinction, as their youth fall under the power of the market. More international dialogue is necessary to understand and influence the impact of Black American popular culture abroad. Since we are far from having the theoretical framework for cultural equity in place, we need to encourage greater debate, writing, and radical thought. The ideas emerging from this process need to take into account national and cultural distinctions in order to create a vision for the future. This vision must then be communicated to the Black communities and their allies as popular concepts, so that they will be broadly accepted and supported. On the practical front, we need to build institutions that are committed to developing leadership in the cultural sphere of our communities' lives. A leadership that seeks to advance the well being of a community will require a break from the opportunism that predominates in the popular culture realm. If we, the leaders of our communities, are engaged in careerism, then the confidence and support that we need will not be forth-coming. When the communities in which we work see us as inte-gral to themselves, we will not have to battle in isolation, as we too often do, thereby falling victim to the divide-and-rule strategy employed by our enemies. In building institutions, we need to cul-tivate successors and a climate of creativity and possibility, to nur-ture involvement and change.

The need for concrete networks is vital for the sharing and exchange of strategies for development. The need for internation-al networks is evident from the fact that the mass media has made the world in effect a global village in which we are all linked. Our need is to forge links that work for our communities. The loss of strong Black institutions of substance, grounded in our communi-ties, is a loss to us all that eats into our confidence, aspirations, and development. We must build Black alliances, even with those institutions with whom we compete for resources or with whom we differ in political interpretation. We will limit the impact our work can have if we do not challenge the many manifestations of racism that continue to be prevalent worldwide. Our negation in the real history of world civilization can only be rectified by our active engagement in reconstruction.

THE PURPOSEFUL UNDERDEVELOPMENT OF LATINO AND OTHER COMMUNITIES OF COLOR

Marta Moreno Vega

In 1992, we, the descendants of the racial and cultural mixing of Native America, Africa, and Spanish Europe, continue to be the victims of white supremacist thought and practice. We are obliged to function in a society that still exalts and develops Europe, while it underdevelops our root cultures through unfair trade and other neocolonial agreements and embargoes. Stateside, our communities are strapped with massive unemployment, homelessness, miseducation, and inadequate medical care, therefore perpetuating and justifying the maginalization of our communities while scattering the potential power of our people. The alarming poverty rate and critical state of health care in our communities reflect the consistent underfunding of organizations meant to reconstruct, transform, and strengthen our communities. Despite these blatant inequities, we continue not only to survive, but to engage in liberating strategies for a future in which we will thrive.

This essay is based on the keynote address delivered to the National Association of Latino Arts and Culture (NALAC) conference on September 25, 1992, in San Francisco.

This conference is an example of our possibilities.

In the late sixties and seventies our communities duplicated what the *cimarrones* (run-away enslaved people) did during colonization. We created safe places for nurturing our cultural and spiritual traditions. We empowered our communities, while establishing locations for resisting Eurocentric cultural oppression. The ancient societies of our ancestors—the *quilombos* of Brazil, the *palenques* of Colombia and Cuba—became the Puerto Rican Traveling Theatre, El Museo del Barrio, Taller Boricua, Galeria de la Raza, Guadalupe Cultural Center, Caribbean Cultural Center, Teatro Campesino, and other cultural-arts-educational organizations too numerous to list. Artists and organizations united and/or collaborated with student movements like the Puerto Rican Student Union, the Young Lords Party, Brown Berets, Movimientos Pro la Independencia de Puerto Rico, and others.

Collectively, we defined, articulated, and insisted upon our fair share of resources, our right to our own culture, and our right to self-determination. We developed ethnic studies programs, Puerto Rican, African American and Chicano studies departments, and culturally grounded institutions that would reconstruct our histories, pass on our traditions, and make visible the creative genius in our communities. It was clear to us that it was necessary to dislocate the imposed *uni*versal Eurocentric hegemonic thought and practice by instituting what Temple University historian C. Tsehloane Keto calls a *pluri*versal cultural vision and practice that placed all of our histories and experiences on an equal level.

The call for social justice, equity and parity carried with it the need for reclamation, reparation, repatriation (when desired), and equitable distribution of decision-making power and resources. Influenced by the Civil Rights and Black Power struggles, our cultural workers produced art that was culturally grounded in the traditions and histories of our people. These expressions gave first voice to our sheroes and heroes who had fought oppression before us. The images of Pedro Albizu Campos, Emiliano Zapata, Julia de Burgos, Pancho Villa, and Emeterio Betances took their places alongside contemporary warriors like Lolita Lebron, Frida Kahlo, Cesar Chavez, Reuben Zalazar, Antonia Pantoja, and other articulators of a new, culturally grounded liberation vision for our communities.

For Puertorriquenos this cultural work meant looking internally. It meant recognizing and affirming our Native and African
identities that for too long had been denied. The words of histori-
an-activist Bernardo Vega were a motivating force: "Without a
doubt, in order to stand on our own two feet, Puerto Ricans of all
generations must begin by affirming our own history. It is as if we
are saying: 'We have roots, therefore we are!'" The indigenous
philosophies and the images of the Tainos and Arawaks as well as
Africa's Yoruba and Kongo became integral to defining and articulating our essential Latino character. The Lukumi and Kongolese
symbols of the Yoruba descendants of Cuba, Santo Domingo, and
Brazil reaffirmed our Africanness just as the *cemies* (triangular
stones representing gods) and other petroglyphs of the Caribbean
Tainos spoke of our Native ancestors. The polyrhythmic communication of the *bata* drums of Cuba, the *tambores minas* of
Venezuela, and the *tambores de bomba* of Puerto Rico also brought
a new cultural language to the surface. These were creative expressions that reflected a holistic dynamism grounded in our Native
and African heritages.

The process of reclaiming, reconstructing, and reaffirming
our cultural centers made it clear that the depth of racial and cultural experiences we embody needed a new aesthetic construct.
Furthermore, this process defined and promulgated our multidi-
mensional levels of experience. We understood what our ancestors
understood: that dance was more than dance, song was more than
song—we understood that, like the drum, these forms were a system of communication, unification, and transformation, developing linkages between our sacred and secular experiences.

The pioneering, culturally grounded arts movement of the
1960s and '70s actively engaged in the transformation of our communities' conditions and the multifaceted international dimension
of our racial and cultural lineages. Together with the Native
American and African American communities, we changed the
society's overt practice of excluding and devaluing our cultural heritages and presence. The pioneering cultural institutions that now
are twenty to thirty years old are the results of our communities'
insistence on developing spaces of nurturing and resistance. These
sacred cultural locations were built by a new leadership in our com-

munities that had no vested interest in maintaining the status quo. El Museo del Barrio in New York City was a school project developed by parents under a state education–sponsored decentralization program; El Taller Boricua was developed by a collective of artists; the Association of Hispanic Arts by a group of Latino organizations. Other institutions were developed by churches, student groups, and community activists, who were framing a new vision and aspiration for our people.

We succeeded, to an extent. We became part of the national dialogue; we became visible. In fact, our numbers made it clear that we were here to stay. It was clear that as a racially and culturally diverse population, our realities had to be addressed within the framework of our cultural experiences and traditions.

Looking back on the process of development of El Museo del Barrio, the Association of Hispanic Arts, the Network of Cultural Centers of Color (which has grown out of collaborative work with racially and culturally diverse organizations, spearheaded nationally by the Caribbean Cultural Center) and now the National Association of Latino Arts and Culture, I note the following: *We underestimated systemic racism and the mindset of dominance that got us here in the first place.* The process of informing, educating, projecting, and practicing a culturally diverse perspective that we felt would dislocate Eurocentrism has been co-opted, redefined, and turned against us by the arts and culture Establishment. The popularization and commodification of cultural diversity has brought forth a recognition of difference, while maintaining the paradigm of dominance and control. Within this framework, the European American status quo continues to disperse the major portions of public and private funds to artists and arts organizations that they have always validated. These institutions are receiving even more funds to reach new audiences (us), and to experiment with "global" projects that blur and decontextualize the definitions of our cultures, while using their criteria for cultural diversity. Simultaneously, the process of destabilizing our artists and cultural organizations continues through the reduction of funding to our communities.

The power remains in the same hands. The justification is the same as it was 500 years ago, albeit less blatant. Our artists and organizations are labeled as *developing, exotic, alternative, underdeveloped, mismanaged, special,* and *community-based.* Any definition will be used to set us in a "less-than" category. This devaluation translates into fewer resources to our artists and organizations. Yet monies magically appear for the Establishment's consultants to technically develop us; as a safeguard against charges of overt discrimination, spots open up for token representation from our communities on their boards of directors and advisory councils. The result is that our art forms are more visible, but they are decontextualized from their historical and cultural frameworks.

The handwriting is on the wall. If we are to save our communities and our cultural life, we must assume the responsibility, as we have done in the past, to publicly and actively claim our rights. We must learn from past experiences and form new strategies to stabilize and expand our resources to our artists, organizations and communities. The *quilombo* spirit of safeguarding our sacred and safe spaces must come to the foreground.

I recommend that this historic gathering of the racial and cultural spectrum that comprises the Latino experience develop proactive strategies, cultivating a movement for Latino cultural equity and parity. Through whatever means necessary we must move collectively to ensure our fair share of representation and resources that reflect our contributions to this country in forced free labor and paid taxes. We must ensure that our cultural spaces survive and thrive for the sake of our young and for all of our futures. If we fail to maintain our cultural grounding, future generations will not be able to speak to their Latino-ness in a liberatory way that is grounded in their ancestral past. The Native American practice of safeguarding and planning for the seventh future generation must also become ours.

We must consider collective legal action to make funders adhere to their philanthropic missions; be prepared to lobby on the federal level and locally for policies and legislation that reflect the interests of our cultural communities; connect our cultural borders through the development of partnerships that expand and enhance our resources; establish systems for exchanging information nationally and internationally to ensure that our root cultures are in line with the thinking of their diaspora populations. I further recommend that we discuss a Cultural Equity Day, not as a day of festival, but as a time to set forth a comprehensive cultural agenda before Congress, which brings the issue of the continued deliberate underdevelopment and exploitation of our communities to the national forefront. Although the United States has withdrawn from UNESCO, we as a community must petition to have our agenda included in the international cultural dialogue for equity.

This conference should not be just a feel-good session; we have attended many of those. This historic conference should forge friendships based on concrete working relationships and create a national and international Latino cultural policy and agenda that protects and advances our collective cultural arts communities. Our communities are in crisis, we know that. We must make this nation aware that we will not allow our continued victimization or that of the cultures we come from. The need for a pluriversal vision and practice grounded in cultural equity must be insisted upon *now*. It is our task to develop strategies and events that say *No Mas* to domination.

LINKING MISSIONS AND RESOURCES ACROSS INTERNATIONAL BOUNDARIES

Esi Sutherland-Addy

In addressing the issue of networking among people of color, my mind turns to the first sixty years of this century, and I acknowledge the efforts of some of the great minds of Africa and its diaspora—their messages reached one another through passionate writings, correspondence, and occasional face-to-face meetings—to share their conviction that African people have a right to be free and to affirm Africa as their homeland. Recall the appearance of *Ethiopia Unbound*, written by Ghana's J. Casely-Hayford in 1911, and W.E.B. DuBois's steady seventy-odd years of prolific writing and activism. The phenomenal rise of Marcus Garvey and his eventful but brief career remains a touchstone in the quest for independence and a dignified life by Africa and its people.

We may also cite movements such as the Back-to-Africa Movement, the Pan-African Movement and the Negritude Movement. These political and cultural movements have recognized and sought to celebrate and to promote the historical continuities among people of African descent. Of equal importance has

This paper was presented as part of a panel, "International Network of Color: Linking Missions, Linking Resources," on October 17, 1991, at the Cultural Diversity Based on Cultural Grounding II Conference in New York City.

been the recognition that, although the exploitation of people of color by Western imperialism may be taking place in different parts of the world, in each case it is simply a different manifestation of the same phenomenon.

It is not surprising, then, to find among the adherents of these movements and ideas people who leaned at least intellectually toward Marxism—a doctrine that seemed to provide the context for recognizing and combating exploitation of human beings by other human beings wherever they might live. Persons with activist inclinations, such as W.E.B. DuBois, Trinidadian Pan-Africanist George Padmore, and Kwame Nkrumah, as well as intellectual Marxists such as Leopold Sedar Senghor, expressed in their work a belief in the linkages generated by common experiences of exploitation.

To suggest a consistent and ever-widening growth of awareness that leads to an improvement in the condition in which people of African descent live, however, is to paint an inaccurate picture.

Although we have known throughout this century that the identification of resources and the linking of missions (purposes and goals) is the only means to achieve a dignified existence, our efforts to make this a reality have been sporadic and ineffectual. Our very presence here today eloquently addresses this situation and the complexity of the position in which we people of color find ourselves.

It is not possible, however, to discuss these issues in a political and economic vacuum. And so, in this paper I shall keep certain political and economic perspectives in view, while promoting the idea that cultural activists must play a number of roles in their society. First, we have to reflect different facets of the human condition in the most poignant way; second, dare to dream aloud, eloquently, in order to paint vivid pictures of what those dreams might be; and third, as the Nigerian writer Isidore Okpewho said in his inaugural lecture at the University of Nigeria at Ibadan in 1990, we have to ensure the establishment of "the creative spirit—the will to make things, *our own things*, among our people." To face our condition today means that we enter into a world of complexity that cannot and must not be underestimated.

Looking at the question of linking missions, we immediately come upon the problems and tensions embodied in a trichotomy of interests: those of states, those of the intellectual and financial elite, and those of the people. Arching over this trichotomy and threatening to destroy it is the international economy.

That people of color live in many different nation-states is a fact that must be reckoned with. I am sure most of us here today—as cultural activists—are basically interested in a "people-to-people" approach. We probably believe that states and their machinery simply hamper the direct interaction of people of color in different parts of the world.

Modern nation-states around the world exist for the most part as a result of a relatively recent, intense, and highly exploitative phase in the history of the world. Today we see a variety of repercussions resulting from this situation. The African continent is balkanized into nonviable states buffeted by the world economy and by the interests of colonial and neocolonial powers. But its leaders at the Organization of African Unity Summit in 1990 set the cautious date of 2023 as the date for unification.

Lack of sovereignty, the economic nonviability of individual nation-states, the world political and economic order, and the role of the elite in politics, business, and academia combine to make statehood an unstable bargain. The need, however, to reformulate the term of nationhood, and using this concept, to provide a stable relationship between people of color and their land, natural resources, and dignity of self cannot be overstated. Neither can people of color afford to forego the opportunities offered by the international political economy for being fully represented in, and taking maximum advantage of, global financial resources to which we contribute on a large scale directly and indirectly.

In regard to current political configurations, then, I can say that disdain for government and therefore attempting to avoid dealing with it is a cop-out and a dissipation of scarce human resources. Not only do we have to learn this lesson, but we must realize that we have to govern ourselves and manage all of our resources. At this time, it is vital that members of the diaspora make strong organizational efforts to counter the current pressures on the governments of small states. The power of exploited people and people of color more generally appears to lie in finding a variety of ways to influence both local and global policy.

Not being a party to policy formulation is not an advantage; it is a clear *disadvantage*. Having said this, it is important to note what is obvious: that people in political office are people, and often, in our countries, they come from groups like the one gathered here. How then shall we complement one another's efforts?

Another part of this trichotomy is ordinary people of color. They are not a homogeneous group, since we find among them different systems of government and social organization and practices, some of which have been and continue to be inimical to progress and development. Of incalculable importance, however, is the fact that among our so-called ordinary people is where we will find what is left of our knowledge of ourselves, our history, our civilization, and the appropriate uses of our environment. We will also find the intellecual tools and aesthetic skills that account for our resilience to adversity. In our effort to identify an overriding link with ordinary people of color, we must be willing to become totally immersed in their quest for a dignified life, with all that this implies in terms of self-determination, provision of basic needs, and holistic development.

Finally the intellectual, and admittedly minute, financial elite among people of color are faced with a series of dilemmas. Often, this elite experiences a tension between their personal aspirations—wanting to participate in and gain recognition and/or financial benefit from the international system centered in the technologically advanced countries—and their knowledge of the needs of the broad majority of their people. It is true that a number of the members of this elite suppress their identification with their people, believing it to be a nonviable sentiment that must be relinquished, in favor of the idea that the world is now a "global village." They feel that they are part of an international community in which skill, competence, and familiarity with with modern technology constitute the requirements for living a decent life. For this reason, those of us who belong to elite groups will work for anyone who pays well for our services.

On the other hand there are those who have a fairly clear perspective on what needs to be done, but as they enter professions, politics, or business, they demonstrate in clear ways individual or class interests that are wholly incompatible with the advancement of their people. Chief among these contradictions is the perpetual claim to speak for and on behalf of the people, instead of helping to create avenues for the people to do and speak for themselves.

Perhaps I have been harsh with the intellectual and financial elite. If I have it is because those of us gathered here form a part of that group and understand who we are as people of color, where we live, what conditions we live under, and what resources are available to us globally. We also have the skills to present possible ways in which people and government might have access to global resources or harness local ones to a set of common purposes. Finally we have the capacity to continue to assist in determining and maintaining perspectives on our common mission.

I should like to draw your attention to a succinct and highly pertinent statement made by Professor Wole Soyinka in last year's DuBois-Padmore-Nkrumah Memorial Lectures at the W.E.B. DuBois Memorial Centre for Pan-African Culture in Accra, Ghana. In his paper, entitled "The Black Man and the Veil: A Century On," Professor Soyinka remarked, "We must yet again underline the existence of tensions beneath this very impulsion [the impulsion to create the virtues of racial dignity and cohesion], a tension of yearning and surrender; of humane commitment and of power hunger; of interrogation and acceptance; of vision and pragmatism; of the purist flame and seductive distractions. In short, of the historic will and its counter inertia. Obviously there would be losses at the areas of tension, and gains. The question was for whom would history be retrieved and reshaped? In whose ultimate interests?"

As I said above, making full use of the international political economy and the global financial resources to which we contribute on a large scale is something we have hardly explored. For example, how many people of color are recognized "experts" in the international network? How many of our sociological, scientific, and cultural projects can be framed in such a way as to extend the scope of United Nations programs, for example, beyond the limitations created by a lack of affinity with those administering them? We also need to mobilize and distribute human resources. Is this goal to be achieved through the establishment of nongovernmental organizations (NGO's) or through existing organizations such as the Caribbean Cultural Center? Again, what are we doing to gain access to international finance and to use it in the interests of people of color? As we organize to mobilize our resources in nontraditional ways, much remains to be done by people who are poor materially, but who together constitute by far the richest group in the world.

Then there is the question of lobbying and consciousness-raising. Many people of color, including those in positions of authority, in academia, and ordinary people, need to be constantly reminded of the condition of our people, our strengths, and our history. Policy makers and public servants require enormous awareness as they create economic policy, or educational policy. They would, however, need common terms of reference. It would be wise to see how documents like the Charter of the Organization of African Unity, the Lagos Plan of Action, the 1990 Abuja Declaration by the Summit of African Heads of State, the United Nations Charter, and the like, can be revisited with a view to keeping our eyes—and the eyes of public servants—on the prize.

Such activities, however, would constitute only one part of a multifaceted approach. Seeing human beings, persons of color, as the center of their own development and that of their people is one approach. The other vital part would be the collection, collation, and dissemination of information about what is happening in the world of people of color and also about how global activities affect people. From the above observation it follows that no effort should be spared in using information to build consciousness and activism. This provides a fascinating area of endless opportunity for cultural activists. It comes with strong challenges, such as targeting particular audiences like children, women, policy makers, young leaders in training, rural populations, and the like.

Much information needs to be adapted and translated into the languages most suited to different audiences. Given the video revolution on the African continent and elsewhere, and the thirst for information, it seems prudent to explore the potential of this medium for reaching a large number of persons with the appropriate messages. It is also vital to stimulate and promote the formation of social groupings around key concepts like holistic development and unity of purpose and to develop a network among such groupings.

Another area in which there has been an appalling lack of interaction is in the area of scholarly work. Too few people of color study and assess the situation of their own people. Those who could be a beacon or provide warning signals can hardly be found outside a very narrow academic space. Where are the collections of essays, collaborative films, scientific research projects, and the student and staff exchanges in academia that would bring to light our concerns? This is surely an area where immediate steps can be taken.

It is an unacceptable fact that in Africa, elite Africans and other elites of color are not at all connected to rural communities and children's needs. It is common to see solitary white missionaries and volunteers in remote villages. Rarely, however, do we see people of color in these villages. This fact of course means that villagers see white benefactors who bring them medicine, water, skills, and religion. Not surprisingly, then, people of color as a whole have little recognition of themselves as an entity and therefore do not benefit from the power of unity of purpose. And so we see that both dissemination of information and activism are essential to address the real needs of the people.

Transferring skills from those who have them to those who do not is a good approach in the area of human resources development. Our people after all are our greatest resource and should be the beneficiaries and the focus of all our efforts. The need to set up systems, therefore, that enable people of color to be effective and self-determining as a group in the world is a task that deserves the fullest attention we can give it.

I have given a summary of my point of view on the question of linking missions and linking resources. As I have indicated above, there is no use denying historical realities, but it would be most self-defeating to seek to uphold the conflicts of the past (for instance, that between Marcus Garvey and W.E.B. DuBois, which posed alleged populism in the case of the former against alleged intellectual elitism on the part of the latter). And, while our mission may need to be redefined because of new developments, in its essence it is the same as it has been for the past 500 years. The obligation to find a way of actualizing the mission by linking social, cultural, political, human, physical, and fiscal resources on a sustained basis now becomes perhaps both our greatest burden and the chief source of our emancipation.

Part III
NEW MEANINGS

AFRICAN AMERICAN CULTURAL EMPOWERMENT

A STRUGGLE TO IDENTIFY AND INSTITUTIONALIZE OURSELVES AS A PEOPLE

Kalamu ya Salaam

Our struggle as African American cultural workers is a struggle not only to win the hearts and minds of our people, it is also a struggle to identify who we are and to institutionalize that identity. The latter process of identification and institutionalization is the critical prerequisite to successfully completing the process of winning hearts and minds.

Strategically, it is important to begin by defining ourselves to ourselves and to promulgate that identity so that it is both accepted by ourselves and respected by others. This process of identification necessitates both distinguishing what makes us who we are and identifying and analyzing the environment that produces us.

The second step is to organize ourselves to institutionalize our culture. We must wage struggle for our own cultural development.

This presentation will offer a definition of our identity as a

This essay was developed from a paper presented at the Cultural Diversity Based on Cultural Grounding Conference in New York City in 1989 and from follow-up meetings in 1990 and 1991.

people and a definition of culture. We will follow the definitions with specific suggestions for ongoing cultural work.

I. DEFINITION: WHO ARE WE AND WHAT IS CULTURE?
IDENTITY

Who are we? The popular term for our people at this moment in history is African American. In the broadest sense of the term any people of African descent who were born and reared in the Western hemisphere are African Americans. The consensus is, however, that *African American* refers specifically to people of African descent born and reared in the United States.

We are a people of deep contradiction on the one hand and internal richness on the other. We have always embodied the critical contradictions of life in America: We were the slave in a country that mythicized itself as the home of the free; we were ineradicably black in a country that idealized whiteness; we were erotic in a country that celebrated Puritanism; and the list goes on. While this contradiction between us as a people and the country within which we were created as a people is the water within which we swim, there is also a deeper contradiction—this is an internal one that most of us never acknowledge, but one that nevertheless significantly affects everything we do as a people.

Our major internal contradiction is the struggle to be ourselves while at the same time striving to become or be accepted by the other. On the one hand, by both nature and social condition, we are the outsider, and on the other hand, because we are the outsider, there is little room in society for us to be who we are. We are trapped in a dilemma: Either we undertake the complex task of being ourselves (that is, both African/Black and American), while being rejected and/or modified by the geo-social matrix that birthed us and, de facto, provided a major part of our identity, or we try, through a combination of persuasion and force, to be accepted by our birth world, and in the process deny or repress much of what we are.

This contradiction of "being and the negation of being" is made more complex by African cultural tendencies toward adaptation to adversity and accommodation of differences as a philosophical mode for resolving conflicts. Manifestations of this "being" contradiction happen not only in the arena of external expressive space, but also, and more complexly, in the arena of our internal imagination. External expressive space encompasses both the physical and social constructs within which one is able to shape the environment to reflect the self; it is concrete and sequential. Internal imagination encompasses the richness (or paucity) of historical, contemporary, and futuristic vision; it is random and abstract.

Because we have had limited external expressive space (when we had any at all), we have a tendency to cling to any opening at the first opportunity. Thus we often express ourselves within social and physical contexts that are often directly contradictory to who we are—but we do so because essentially that is the only opportunity.

Although our history as Africans predates and significantly contributes to our overall identity, it is essentially true that our history as a *particular* people, as African Americans, began in the crucible of chattel slavery. Within this crucible our various African ethnicities were, through external forces, ground into a unique, complex, and often contradictory identity. Although we gestated for approximately two centuries in the crucible of chattel slavery, which served as our womb of fetal growth, we were not actually born as a people until the period between the end of the Civil War and the beginning of the Great Depression, when, for the first time in the American portion of our history, the great masses of us were able to begin to shape a world of our own making.

It is no accident that Reconstruction is the period when all of our music was codified into the world-respected genres of blues, gospel, and jazz. This was the period of the formation of most of our major self-determined social, political, and economic organizations and tendencies. This was the period when we, as a people on a national level, first asserted ourselves. Although we have been here since 1619, our self-directed development in terms of external expressive space only began, on a mass level, in this period, the late 1800s. Sometimes we completely forget that two-thirds of our time on American shores has been spent as chattel slaves who were unable to assert ourselves externally.

Our compensation for the denial of external expressive space was, of course, the development of an unprecedented internal rich-ness, which found numerous creative outlets—usually in ways that left no physical leavings behind as evidence that might be used against us by our oppressors. The centuries-old denial and dis-ruption of external expressive space has resulted in an inbred ten-dency toward ephemeral external expressiveness—in the arts we "prefer" music and orature (actually, it is not a preference, but rather is the result of a survival strategy).

When people talk about our oral nature and point to African antecedents, they are only partially correct. Consider that in the visual arts, African sculpture is not only the preeminent influence on twentieth-century Western visual arts (via the cubists), but the prevalence of sculpture as a form of artistic expression is also char-acteristic of all West African peoples, the source peoples of the vast majority of African Americans. Among African American artists, however, sculpture is not a major mode of expression.

Our reality is complex. African oral traditions were easily adaptable to the social strictures of chattel slavery and hence could be retained and even expanded upon without compromising one's survival. Although the colonizer and the enslaver forbade the use of African languages, they could not forbid the Africanizing of European languages by Africans who were forced to speak those languages. Sculpture, on the other hand, could not be retained in a similar way.

The external expressive space of language was thereby bifur-cated: Among ourselves we spoke English in one way, and between ourselves and the others we spoke English in another way. Unlike other ethnic groups, such as Italian immigrants, who spoke Italian in the home and English in the street, our contradiction was that we were never allowed the expressive space, even within our homes, to speak our African languages. Thus, no matter how much we Africanized the English language, we were still caught in the outsider dilemma.

Visual imagery, especially Afrocentric sculpture, did not become a critical mode of artistic expression on a national level until the turn of the twentieth century, when it was relatively safer to assert the African self. Before then the colonizer and enslaver systematically prohibited the production of and destroyed all visual imagery of the African self. This prohibition and destruction did not mean that our enslaved ancestors did not want to or were not capable of physically imaging themselves through the visual arts, rather this meant that we were prevented from expressing ourselves. This point may seem redundant, but in too many cases, even among ourselves, we interpret the seeming absence of an action or product to mean failure of either the will or the ability to do the action or produce the product.

The result of external prohibitions and destruction of concrete Afrocentric self-expression was an interruption in the cultural continuity of passing on Afrocentric aesthetics and techniques, which is why much of our "concrete" artwork often starts out as emulative of existing models, rather than from a self-expressive basis. In opposition, our "ephemeral" artwork, specifically our music and orature, generally represents an innovative, creative synthesis, which accurately expresses the complex identity of the "new" people now called African Americans.

These examples serve to illustrate the complexity of our ever-evolving task of external and internal definition, one that was notably advanced by W.E.B. DuBois in his important work, *The Souls of Black Folk*. He noted:

...the Negro is a sort of seventh son, born with a veil, and gifted with second-sight in this American world, —a world which yields him no true self-consciousness, but only lets him see himself through the revelation of the other world. It is a peculiar sensation, this double-consciousness, this sense of always looking at one's self through the eyes of others, of measuring one's soul by the tape of a world that looks on in amused contempt and pity. One ever feels his two-ness, — an American, a Negro; two souls, two thoughts, two unreconciled strivings; two warring ideals in one dark body, whose dogged strength alone keeps it from being torn asunder. The history of the American Negro is the history of this strife, — this longing to attain self-conscious manhood, to merge his double self into a better and truer self.

The identity question is critical at this time, precisely because for the first time in the history of America, there is a major shift in both the reality and the perception of the ethnic makeup of the United States. The media frequently comments on what is called the "browning" or "colorizing" of America, which is really a recognition of shifting balances of power, rather than simply of a shift in ethnic makeup. The truth is that America has always been a country of color, even though Europeans vainly tried to turn it into an Eden of whiteness. Not without some resistance and without fully coming to grips with its history of color and color suppression, America is resigning itself to the fact that its future is multicultural, multiethnic. The future is not white. For African American artists and art producers the immediate future offers, for the first time in our history in this country, an unprecedented opportunity for the development of expressive external space within which our Black identity can be documented, expressed, and celebrated.

The turn of the century, under segregation, saw the development of external expressive space within Black communities nationwide, but there was no comparable opening in society at large. The 1990s offers us an opening in society at large, albeit under the less than ideal conditions of the near total destruction of functional Black communities. The paradox is that when we could operate from a home space, we had no, or limited, access to national space. Now that access to national space is opening up, we are witnessing the simultaneous devolution and dissipation, indeed the near total destruction, of our home spaces. Our residential areas (our home living spaces) are decimated and corrupted by social problems ranging from rampant unemployment, miseducation, and inadequate or nonexistent health care, to drugs, crime, and political corruption. The severity of our home problems notwithstanding, the nineties are a period of opportunity to *expand* our access to external expressive space.

The opportunities of this time period give an even greater urgency to our task of defining ourselves, precisely because our self-definition no longer is severely restricted by the definitions of us by others—now we have the opportunity to begin being and defining ourselves.

CULTURE

What is culture? Some people loosely define culture as the arts: as both the modes of expression of the arts and the products and artifacts produced by artists. This is what I call the artistic definition of culture. Others define culture as the total lifestyle of a definable group of people. This definition, whether proposed by anthropologists, social scientists, or political scientists, posits culture as the sum total of daily existence, codified by values and social systems established to pass on values and perpetuate a given social order. This is what I call the life-style definition of culture.

Typically, "artistic-culture" adherents accuse "life-style-culture" adherents of relegating the arts to being a minor determinant in the course of human development, and vice versa, life-style culture adherents accuse artistic culture proponents—because they tend to almost exclusively concentrate on the arts—of being so narrow that they overlook or exclude the deterministic forces of economics, politics, and social organization as major forces that shape culture.

I think it is important to start with a broad definition and, appropriate to the point of discussion, follow up by focusing on a specific area of culture: *Culture is a concrete manifestation of the collective values and behavior that define a social group. It is maintained by individuals acting through institutions and ideologies that defend and develop the culture.*

Maulana Karenga (the architect of the Black nationalist philosophy of Kawaida and the founder of the African American holiday, Kwanzaa) is fundamentally correct when he notes, "To have a culture, a people must be aware of that culture, accept it, and practice it." Awareness can be either reflexive or reflective, that is, one does what one has been nurtured to like and accept (reflexive) or does what one thinks ought to be done (reflective). Although the majority of cultural activity is reflexive rather than reflective, it is nonetheless done out of an awareness that the culture exists. Moreover, awareness can be unconscious (intuitive) or self-conscious (reasoned). Intuitive awareness is usually based on repetitions of experience, and one generally receives it by being reared in an environment that teaches and validates specific behavior. When we dance to popular music (a reflexive act), we may not be aware that we are exhibiting a cultural manifestation, but we are aware that we are dancing. When we decide to learn how to do a specific dance step or style, we have then moved into the area of reasoned (reflective) awareness.

One of the critical tasks of the cultural worker is to specialize in the reflective awareness of culture. A major aspect of this activity is the practical defining of culture.

Karenga has proposed seven criteria of culture. This is important because one cannot accurately study that which is not defined in an orderly fashion. How can we interpret the world and our place within the world without consciousness, without a world view? Moreover, when we don't develop our own definitions and viewpoints, inevitably and unconsciously we will assume and use the definitions and viewpoints of the dominant society within which we are reared.

Karenga's seven criteria of culture (along with my brief definition of each) are:

1. *Mythology*. The explanation of existence.

a. Philosophy — human attempts to answer why a thing or being exists.

b. Religion — socially organized attempts at defining the proper relationship between things, beings, and the universe, based on a value system (that is, a codification of right and wrong in both the ideal and the social context).

c. Science — systematic attempts to discover the laws of nature that govern all material things.

2. *History*. A systematic examination and analysis of the relevance of the past activities of a group as both subject and object of those activities.

3. *Social Organization*. The way in which daily relationships, especially involving procreation, marriage, childrearing, education, health care, and death are self-consciously structured.

4. *Political Organization*. The ways in which we organize to gain, maintain, and use power, especially our forms of self-governance and self-defense.

5. *Economic Organization*. The system of ownership, production, and distribution of labor, material resources, and goods and services.

6. *Creative Motif*. The ways in which we beautify or reinterpret reality through reorganization of matter (for example, producing and ordering sound in order to make music).

7. *Ethos*. A defining or identifying characteristic of a people or an era. For example, *the sixties, the Harlem Renaissance*, and *the Depression* are shorthand designations to describe a set of dominant or guiding beliefs or attitudes and/or social life-styles.

For peoples of color in twentieth-century America, defining a particular people's culture is complicated both by the legacy of systemic oppression and exploitation and by the profoundly far-reaching forces of the global marketplace. The dominant force in today's global marketplace is Western commodity-based popular culture. From this perspective we see two major forces at work: the dominant political and economic conditions within which peoples live, and their reactions to those conditions, especially their conscious actions to change the conditions; and the relationship of a particular people's culture to Western commodity-based popular culture. From my perspective, there are two major lines of demarcation that must be addressed. One is the question of control of the economic and political forces that are the basic structure of any culture. The other is the distinction between popular and national culture.

The Control Of Culture. Of the seven criteria of culture, politics and economics generally exert the greatest, but not always the most determinant, influences. Moreover, in the context of the cultures of peoples of color in the Western hemisphere, it is equally important to analyze and understand the politics and economics of the dominant (and often dominating) culture, in order for us to fully understand our own cultures of color. Politics is the most self-conscious expression of culture, precisely because politics is always about power, always about who will be in charge of the society and to what degree they will control it. In the modern marketplace, the political orientation of the artist (that is, opposition to or accommodation to the dominant political forces) is often as important as the quality of the artistic work.

Economics is the single most important spur and/or impediment to the development of culture, because the economic system, in conjunction with the political system, either rewards or punishes artistic expression.

In subsistence and rural economies, raw labor is often sufficient to insure survival. In a modern, urban industrial economy, however, it takes money to survive, regardless of one's labor. The market forces become the major censure in modern free enterprise societies, often more effective than the censure of the police state, because an artist who cannot "earn" a living becomes dependent on others for a source of income.

Obviously, successful contemporary artists are those who quickly learn to shape their artwork so that they might support themselves by selling the goods and services they produce as artists. Some view this self-selected "educational process" as selling out artistic integrity to the bottom line, others view the process as the inevitable pragmatism of life choices. Regardless, the point is that rather than prohibit any specific expressive form or content, the marketplace forces each artist who wants to be successful to make a choice regarding artistic expression. In this way, modern society can present itself as liberal and based on freedom of expression, while actually offering a very narrow window for cultural expression.

Moreover, in twentieth-century America, how one deals economically becomes the central political question: how one earns one's living, what one does with one's earnings, and who and what one voluntarily supports financially—these are the real political measuring rods.

National Culture And Popular Culture. The two major forms of culture are national and popular culture. National culture is the reflective, self-conscious, idealistic advocacy of a particular people's culture by the people themselves, through their cultural leadership (which includes artists, political leaders, and social leaders) with financial support from individuals and institutions of that culture. Although it does not exclude outside support, self-support is a sine qua non of national culture. Popular culture is the semi- or unconscious reflexive presentation of a people's culture as entertainment and/or in the form of commodities for sale.

National culture may or may not have commercial value, but because its purpose is to make a point rather than make a sale, politics is more important than economics (although the role of economics is never to be considered negligible). Popular culture may or may not make a political point, but because its purpose is to make money rather than move people to think and act, economic considerations are more important than politics (although the political system often dictates what is to be economically rewarded).

An example will clarify this issue, I hope. Symphonic music is a national cultural expression of the United States's dominant culture. It is supported at a significantly higher level of public and private institutional funding than all of the other musical forms combined. The system supports symphonic music. Jazz, on the other hand, is viewed by the dominant society as a popular-culture form and thus receives less than 10 percent of the public funds and in-kind support given to symphony music. Another way to put it is: If symphonic music had to make it on drinks and admissions at the door, as jazz music often does, there would not be one functioning symphonic orchestra in America.

Although even a cursory analysis of jazz will show it is more reflective of the American reality and the American ideals of democracy and individual achievement, jazz is nevertheless viewed as a popular cultural expression and thus left to fend for itself in the marketplace, though it is judged worldwide as America's single most important contribution to world culture.

The majority of symphonic music performed by American orchestras is music written by Europeans and unashamedly celebrates historic European cultural realities. The majority of jazz compositions performed by jazz ensembles in America was written by Americans and celebrates historic American cultural realities. Nevertheless, the symphonic orchestras that perform essentially European music receive the vast majority of all public monies allocated for music. They receive the bulk of national, regional, state and local grants, subsidies, and endowments.

It is essential to any understanding of the distinction between national and popular culture that one have an ideology (or world view) that equips one not only to see the cultural realities, but also to understand the forces at work that support their maintenance and discourage change of the status quo. In this context, the status quo support of symphonic orchestras and the nonsupport of jazz reflects cultural imperialism. Thus, the struggle to change this status quo in order to achieve the status and support for jazz that it deserves is essentially a political struggle in support of a national art form, albeit an art form that was created by a colonized and formerly enslaved people.

The maintenance of European-based classical music as the national music of America is an act of racism and imperialism, precisely because it upholds Eurocentric dominance in a non-European context. Without a doubt, jazz is an American invention, birthed by, and on a creative level, largely fueled by the innovations of African Americans. The African American origins and dominant influences of jazz, in combination with the federal government's tacit cultural Eurocentrisim, account for the relative neglect of jazz at the national level.

Today, in the late twentieth century, Great Black Music (that is, gospel, blues, jazz, rhythm and blues, and all of their offshoots) is the leading musical art form of American culture, even though the arbiters of American culture are more interested in eighteenth- and nineteenth-century European music than twentieth-century American music (whether jazz or classical, for that matter). This is the case precisely because the main arbiters of American culture espouse a colonialist mentality and see themselves as upholding the standards of so-called civilization.

Amilcar Cabral, a West African anticolonial leader and internationally respected liberationist intellectual, correctly analyzed that the espousal and development of national culture is necessarily and undeniably an act of national liberation within the context of cultures of oppressed people. To extend Cabral's insight, it is possible then to understand why the advocates of national culture tend to put politics in the lead and the advocates of popular culture tend to put economics in the lead.

National culture is reflective-introspective and popular culture is reflexive-projective. Like a mirror, popular culture simply shows us what's happening at the moment. National culture goes beyond merely mirroring reality to analyze not only what is happening but why; it also offers a vision of what ought to happen and a comparison of what is happening to what has happened historically and what is possible in the future.

National culture emphasizes understanding. Popular culture emphasizes experiencing. *To be* Black and to *understand* Black are two different things. Moreover, experience is not a substitute for knowledge. Many persons can experience something and never understand or be able to articulate what it is.

National culture is literate and popular culture is oral. Sometimes we make the mistake of presenting ourselves as an oral people and thus assume there is no need for documentation. But historically, even so-called oral people had ways in which they documented their culture for purposes of preservation and propagation. Many oral-based cultures also were very sophisticated in their employment of symbols and images used in both religious and utilitarian ceremonies and on sacred objects and everyday artifacts, such as statues, housing, clothing, and cooking utensils.

Literate does not mean writing in English. I mean by it employing a means of documentation that is not subjective, not dependent on the memory of any individual person or small group of people. Although *literate* generally means being able to read and write, for the purposes of this discussion, a literate society is one in which there is documentation of the culture in a mechanical form. Ideally, the national literature should be democratic, meaning that it is technologically accessible to the masses of the people. For example, recordings are not a written form, but they are a valuable means of documentation. Only that which is documented can be studied and passed on to "all" of the people. The problem with a nondocumented culture is not only that it is difficult to pass on, but it is also inherently undemocratic. In those cases, knowledge becomes concentrated in the minds of a few, while the majority go through life being ignorant.

Thus, we have addressed the questions of identity and culture. The opportunity exists for us to advance the ongoing development of an African American national culture, as well as the concomitant development of cultural institutions necessary to document, propagate, and nurture our national culture.

The following are a few suggestions for African American cultural development in this period of incipient American multiculturalism.

SUGGESTIONS FOR CULTURAL WORK

Defining, documenting, and propagating an African American national culture ought to be our major objective.

1. Our first step ought to be networking and meeting to work at establishing a common tongue, a common language with a shared set of definitions.

This first step necessarily must include periodic meetings and symposia at which questions are raised and discussed. What is to be our response to the opening created by the acceptance of "multiculturalism"? How are we to maximize our gains and minimize our losses that will result from mainstream cultural institutions becoming actively involved in "multicultural programming"? How can we influence, if not direct, the defining of multicultural policymaking on a national level? How are we to actively coalesce among ourselves as artists and arts producers representing the various cultures of color in America?

I am not proposing answers to these questions, rather I am suggesting a way to facilitate generating the answers. It is the responsibility of all of us involved at the leadership level of this process to use existing mechanisms to get this work done. Whatever conferences, symposia, and speaking engagements we can actively influence, we should do so, to make sure that multiculturalism issues are raised at every such meeting and that key members of our movement are invited to present.

That is the first step forward: getting together to establish working definitions. A working definition is a beginning point for ongoing development rather than an absolute, carved in stone for all time. Critical to this process is writing down and disseminating our working definitions, including the rationale for them.

Our specific task in this regard is *to create and share a self determined glossary of multiculturalism*.

2. We must continue (by both deepening and broadening) the process of documenting our national culture. We should begin identifying methods for documenting our cultures, begin identifying available and potential resources to use in the documentation effort, and especially we should begin building networks to distribute our documentation.

It is not nearly as easy to recruit committed people to get

actively involved in the process of documenting our culture as it is to get those same people involved in organizing or participating in conferences and festivals. Of course, writing a paper and organizing a panel are significantly easier than editing a book or producing a videotape, but ultimately the process of documentation is more important.

The documentation can be passed on infinitely and can also become an arsenal for use by other cultural warriors around the world, as they wage the ongoing battle to establish national cultures liberated from the cultural imperialism dominant in the world today.

Our second specific task is *to document our national culture from both a performance-presentation and a philosophical-analytical basis*.

3. We need to develop specific strategies to support existing cultural institutions and to work, in a coproducing capacity, with existing "mainstream" cultural institutions. Although such a strategy may seem to be common sense on the surface, there is no existing program in place to promote this "common sense" strategy.

We need to meet and hammer out specific guidelines for institutional development. For example, we can consider establishing a directory of major cultural institutions of color and promoting membership in those institutions. We can begin to monitor producing, curatorial, and high-level administrative positions that become available in "mainstream" cultural institutions and actively lobby to place selected individuals in those positions, to facilitate developmental linkages between those mainstream institutions and our own cultural institutions of color. In essence I am calling for us to go beyond mere survival. Now is the time for us *to develop strategies for cultural development*.

These suggestions by no means exhaust the list of what we should be doing—in fact, they are meant only as a starting point. We are in a phase of victory precisely because the mainstream culture is in a period of crisis. Now is the time to move boldly forward into a future that we actively work to create.

Cultural empowerment for people of color is a major struggle, a struggle that, in many critical ways, will be the inspiration for ongoing specific political and economic development. As cultural workers, primarily in the sphere of artistic work, we are responsible for uplifting the imaginative power of our people. Our product is a product of our imaginations, and it will be through the use of our creative potential that we will find a way forward.

Let us move forward. Let ART FOR LIFE! be our watchwords.

CULTURAL PLURALISM

A GOAL TO BE REALIZED

Antonia Pantoja and Wilhelmina Perry

For many of us who grew up in the United States and Puerto Rico during the 1930s and 1940s, the concept of cultural diversity invokes childhood memories of school activities such as plays, class projects, songs, and recitations. We were too young and naive to ask why our culture was not celebrated. As we were educated through songs about the great contributions of European cultures, we simultaneously learned that our own cultures were inferior and had contributed nothing to the advancement of civilization. Cultural diversity referred to someone else's culture. It was never associated with the culture of Afro-Americans or Puerto Ricans. Because we were young and did not have the tools to fight back, often we internalized these seeds of inferiority.

Today, we are experiencing a sudden reemergence of the concept of cultural diversity, and people of color are being asked to make contributions. Our contributions will be based upon the political and historical awareness that we acquired during the 1960s and 1970s. At that time we, the unequal and disenfranchised, discovered some bitter, but important facts. One realization was that annual celebrations of an event or figure of our history are effective methods of diverting our attention from the political, economic, social, and cultural resources, essential to our well-being, which were being withheld from us. In other words, the ideology of cul-

This paper is based on a presentation made to the Cultural Diversity Based on Cultural Grounding Conference in 1989 in New York City.

tural diversity has been reduced to meaningless one-day celebrations that have in no way changed our situation of inequality. We also discovered that although there are other groups within society that are considered different as well, their differences award them a major share of the available political, social, economic, and cultural resources. This is because their differences are assigned superior values by society. These realities shaped our understanding of cultural diversity.

It is important to understand why the concept of cultural diversity is being recycled now. As the outsiders, we must ask ourselves whether this is just assimilation in a new package. Is this a new method to deny us political power and to control the definition of who we are while ignoring our needs? Does the shifting United States population require a new form of political neocolonialism? Is this diversity just another effort to teach the privileged and professional classes about people of color so that they can use this information in ways that will more effectively service themselves artistically, culturally, and philosophically?

In *Workforce 2000: Work and Workers for the 21st Century*, the United States Department of Labor projects a work force in which white males, "thought of only a generation ago as the mainstays of the economy, will comprise only 15 percent of the net additions to the labor force between 1985 and 2000. By 2010, one in every three eighteen-year-olds will be Black or Hispanic, compared to one in five in 1985."[1]

The complete picture is one of change where large numbers of non-European immigrants from Africa, Asia, South and Central America, and the Caribbean will constitute majorities in many major cities. These immigrants will contribute to existing social movements. Many of these new immigrants are skilled workers and professionals, and these qualities will be highly valued in a changing United States economy. They come from countries with a history of democratic civil struggles and political revolutions. They arrive with a strong sense of cultural and ethnic identity within their intact family and social networks and strong ties to their home countries. At the same time they have a strong determination to achieve their goals, and they do not intend to abandon or relinquish their culture as the price for their success.

They will be needed in a new economy, and they will demand better terms for their contributions. The outdated concept of assimilation, with its systems of reward and punishment, will be useless in persuading them to aspire to idealized white Anglo-Saxon norms. Today, traditional patterns of domination cannot be sustained.

At this time, when people of color with origins outside Europe constitute the majority in many of the urban centers of the United States, we must not be deceived by false concepts or by well-intentioned liberals. We must accept no less than economic, social, cultural, and political parity. Efforts toward the celebration of diversity must work hand-in-hand with the quest for democracy for all citizens of the society. If this is not accomplished, diversity remains a series of meaningless acts that reveal aspects of our uniqueness without challenging or requiring that those in power address important issues.

To continue the analysis of our present concerns and our apprehensions about the present implementations of the concept of cultural diversity, other questions arise that must be addressed if we are to arrive at clear, intelligent conclusions. Are we to believe that the dominant group's position of cultural diversity is honest and in our best interests when there is a national movement that would deny non-English speakers the right to speak their native languages; when people of color and members of gay communities are experiencing revived political disenfranchisement and violent physical attacks; when a movement, cloaked in religion and patriotism, is pressing people to conform to its tenets; and when anti-Japanese sentiments are recycled to offset and affix blame for a sagging United States economy in world markets? We must ask whose diversity is being celebrated; toward what ends; and from what political ideology? The authors accept cultural diversity as a descriptive concept identifying the situation of the United States with its multiple populations. However, we reject cultural diversity as a policy position because, politically, it is a concept of the ideology of assimilation and will sustain current economic and political systems. We adopt the concept of cultural pluralism, rather than cultural diversity, as a way to project an ideology for a truly democratic society.

We bring to this discussion our participation in the cultural pluralism movement of the 1960s and 1970s. Significant among the advocates of cultural pluralism were people of color, people of European descent, women, homosexuals, senior citizens, the disabled, religious communities, and groups with alternative lifestyles. That movement had, at its core, the aspiration to create a new society, where culturally different groups could exist and fully experience both the positive and distinctive attributes of their differences without the penalties of loss of status or economic, educational, social, or political disenfranchisement.

DEFINITIONS OF CULTURAL PLURALISM

The concept of cultural pluralism has been in existence in the United States for approximately sixty years. During this time, many efforts have been made to analyze the status of intergroup relations in our society and to offer an alternative societal model. Early writers on this subject have included Horace M. Kallen, Gunnar Myrdal, Tamot se Shibutani, Milton Gordon, Robert Blauner, and Albert Memmi.

For the purpose of examining the evolution of this concept, we have included definitions that we think most approximate a dynamic understanding of cultural pluralism. Since these definitions were written, many significant events occurred that have shaped a new social movement of cultural pluralism. An increasing number of cultural communities are appearing in the United States. These new groups, whose unifying base has not been ethnicity or race, are demanding the right and opportunity to function as distinctive communities within our society. The definitions that follow predate these changes.

The definition of cultural pluralism set forth by Horace M. Kallen in 1915 envisioned a multiethnic European nation residing within an American civilization that utilized English as a common language.[2]

Frank Bonilla, a sociologist on the faculty of the City University of New York, contended that within the United States, cultural pluralism would seem to mean sharing economic and political institutions while maintaining different cultures. However, pluralism would be meaningless for groups outside the mainstream unless anchored in institutions with the requisite resource and power base to create an appropriate framework for the long-term maintenance of these cultural foundations.[3]

Subsequent studies further expanded the definition of cultural pluralism to include the diversity of new and nonethnic groups.

In our continuing quest for a pluralistic democracy, we must proceed by addressing three significant processes: the relationship of those in power to the disenfranchised; the relationship of various disenfranchised groups to one another; and the relationship of the disenfranchised to themselves.

During the late 1970s Pantoja and Perry attempted to capture the values and objectives of the culturally diverse human-rights movement in an expanded operational definition of cultural pluralism:

> Cultural pluralism is the condition in a society in which individuals, on the basis of ascribed or attained characteristics, are able to form and develop communities along the differences of race, age, sex, religion, language, and cultural life styles. These communities are open systems and members can select to belong to one or more communities at the same time. This condition can only exist in a society where there are two or more culturally diverse functioning communities, and where these communities adhere to a universal value that promotes the use of the resources of the society to fulfill the needs of all of its members. This condition is considered realized in a society where culturally different communities exist, are recognized and permitted to participate and to control those functions and resources which they consider vital to their community's functioning. Cultural pluralism cannot exist in a society where culturally different communities exist in isolation from each other and/or in competition under unequal conditions for the life sustaining/life enhancing resources that the society produces.[4]

To provide the reader with clarity in understanding cultural pluralism redefined, we will further examine and discuss the concepts of culture, community, and life enhancing resources. We define the concept of culture in the sociological and anthropological sense: the basic social habits, products, emotions, attitudes, and values of any group of people. From the point of view of the individual, culture may be defined as any behavior that he or she has learned in conformity with the standards of a particular group. This group may be family, associates, coworkers, religious sects, political parties, or all of the above combined. Also expressed in this perspective, culture includes the communicative, essential values and the material components of a given community's way of life. All these components form a cohesive life style for a group of people.

In order to provide boundaries for observing emerging social units, we are also presenting our definition of community. A community is a group of people who come together to create the processes, institutions, and relationships that function to meet their needs as they define them. Binding elements may include the locality, biological and social characteristics, or shared experiences, language, social needs, and circumstances.

Inasmuch as several cultural communities may exist within the context of a total society, the multiple needs of individuals may be met in one or several communities. Needs that cannot be met in primary or smaller units may be met through the social institutions and processes that are utilized by all members of a given society.

In our definition of cultural pluralism, we are using the term *life-sustaining and enhancing resources* with the intention of identifying the full scope of goods and services that meet people's needs. We differentiate this from the term *social services* as generally used by policy makers and professionals to identify the basic services required by the poor and the dependent. It is our belief that the poor, the infirm, and all the citizens of our society are entitled to life-sustaining and life-enhancing resources, which we identify as food, health, education, clean air, water, shelter, and the array of resources to sustain a good quality of life.

Nonmaterial needs are related to peoples' spiritual, aesthetic, psychological, and intellectual nature. These include the need for dignity, love, belonging, security, expression, and fulfillment; the need to find sources and solutions to problems; the need for relationships with others; the need to locate oneself in time, place and context; and the need to exercise the power required to achieve desired goals.

Human society was created to fulfill both of these types of needs. However, racism, sexism, economic exploitation, and unplanned technological growth have destroyed the effectiveness of the social institutions originally designed to meet these needs. The resulting sense of alienation, powerlessness, and social and economic abandonment have become the foundation for newly emerging, culturally different communities.

Cultural pluralism, as we have described it, does not currently exist in our society. Instead, we have a society of different cultural groups living together under conditions of competition, hostility, and polarization. The competition has its origin in the struggle for the life-sustaining and life-enhancing resources and for opportunities to participate in decision making. Groups achieve varying degrees of success in this competition. Some achieve it at the expense of others, while others achieve almost no success. The struggle is a result of a society of inequality—the inequality of opportunities and of outcomes. This drama has been so institutionalized through social policies, processes, and relationships that it has become a way of thinking and functioning: an ideology, rather than an arrangement that is organized and implemented by a specific, identifiable group of people. Many members of the authors' own ethnic groups reject the premise that other groups experience deprivation and exclusion within this society. We disagree. Conditions of oppression are experienced by many groups within our society, although the manifestations and degrees of oppression may vary.

THE MYTH OF CULTURAL SUPERIORITY

Blauner observes in *Racial Oppression in America*:

Culture and social organizations are important as vessels of a people's autonomy and integrity; when cultures are whole and vigorous, conquest, penetration and certain modes of control are more readily resisted.[5]

The myth of cultural superiority has been connected to the economics of colonialism. Although the economic basis of colonialism has changed, historically world powers, including the United States, have required large pools of unskilled labor to expand and industrialize. These pools of people, who become both the workers and the consumers of goods, are the colonized: the immigrants and people of color living within the boundaries of the country. When outright military controls are impractical, value systems and policies are used to sustain the existing economic power base. The myth of superiority serves those in power who construct a rationale for exercising authority over others that becomes acceptable to society and, ultimately, becomes credible to those whom it subjugates.

These concepts, and the policies, programs, and services that support them, allow the dominant group to exercise authority over decision making and resource allocation. These institutionalized policies and allocating processes become the system by which disenfranchised groups compete with one another and shape and mold themselves in order to receive the rights and privileges of the larger society. For, without these myths, the subjugated and excluded would become conscious of their situation and would have the capacity to reject their domination.

PREFERRED vs. UNPREFERRED GROUPS

The first steps toward achieving a social change as difficult as cultural pluralism are to recognize the existing situation and to admit that change is needed.

Figures 1 and 2 present a model for the analysis of the present situation and the manner in which it is institutionalized. The model can also serve as a useful tool in moving the unpreferred groups in our society from hostile competition to an understanding of their commonly shared situations, thereby creating the basis for the establishment of coalitions. This is an important goal to attain since coalitions are a necessary prerequisite to moving toward cultural pluralism.

Figure 1
PREFERRED CHARACTERISTICS

CHARACTERISTICS	REWARDS
Race: White	Power, Control Over Resources, Opportunities, and Wealth
Power Role*: Colonizer, Owner of Wealth, Oppressor	Decision-makers
Culture: Anglo-Saxon Language: Standard English Religion: Protestant Values: Competitiveness, Individualism, Political Liberalism	Wealth or High Income Leisure and Best Jobs Well-Educated, University Degree Laws Give Preferential Treatment
Sex: Male	Holder of Privileges
Sexual Preference: Heterosexual	Free Access to Potential Partners
Age: Adulthood through Middle Age	Value Setters, Behavior Definers
Social Class: Upper and Middle	Controllers of Knowledge and Communication
Geographic origins: Non-Rural (except Landowners), Non-Southern	

White Anglo-Saxon males control an economic system based on inequality. They own the means of production, and they control the state and its political institutions.

*"Power Role" is defined as the position that one assumes or inherits, or that is delegated to someone in the society.

Figure 2
UNPREFERRED CHARACTERISTICS

CHARACTERISTICS	PUNISHMENTS
Race: Nonwhite	Dependency, Powerlessness, Resourcelessness
Power Role: Object of Colonialization in Country of Origin and/or in the U.S.	Disenfranchisement (Economic, Political, Social), Oppression
Culture: Non-Anglo-Saxon	Poor Education or None
Language: Non-English Speaker or Speaker of Non-Standard English	Object of Misinformation and/or Lack of Information
Religion: Non-traditional Protestant, Catholic, Non-Christian	Religious Discrimination
Values: Collectivism, Group Solidarity, Political Radicalism and Conservatism	Inequality Before the Law
Sex: Female, Sexual Preference: Heterosexual Age: Child, Youth, Senior	Object of Discrimination, Ridicule, and/or Persecution
Social Class: Lower, Poor	Unemployment, Seasonal Employment, Undesirable Jobs
Geographic Origins: Rural; Urban Inner Cities	Landlessness, Homelessness

People of color who may also be immigrants from colonized nations inhabit rural and urban slums, which suffer from poverty and its accompanying economic and social ills. They are the unequal of the nation, and its institutions deny them services, resources, legal protection, and access. They are the majority of the sick, the mentally ill, the imprisoned, and the homeless.

The United States uses specific criteria for identifying the characteristics that establish preferredness or unpreferredness. This criteria includes race, power roles, culture, language, religion, gender, sexual preference, values, age, social class, and geography. Characteristics of preferredness represent the norm and are rewarded, while characteristics of unpreferredness elicit punishment.

Characteristics of preferredness in our society (see Figure 1) are embodied most in the white Anglo-Saxon Protestant male. There is a direct correlation between the number of preferred characteristics and an individual's opportunities to attain rewards. Preferredness, therefore, is a matter of degree. An understanding of the nature and manifestation of discrimination and oppression is necessary to ensure that certain populations within this society attain access to needed resources. For example, white males who may openly identify themselves as gay will not share in the same privileges as other white males. This has also been the situation for other whites from Southern and Eastern European ethnic groups, who comprise the majority of the white working class. In another example, Puerto Rican and African American males, who are unpreferred and thereby suffer, still fare better than the women of their respective ethnic groups when it comes to compensation for wages, awarding of privileges, and the ability to exercise power. Success is measured as the sum total of rewards and privileges enjoyed by the most preferred members of the society: the wealthy and the policy makers.

We have asked the reader to consider cultural pluralism as an approach that respects, includes and demands equal rights, access, and resources for all communities with respect for their cultural and national origins. It is important to do this now because at this time in our history, we must reformulate our concept of cultural diversity. The model of preferredness and unpreferredness has been included here to facilitate our understanding of this issue and to help us arrive at a clear analysis that can distinguish between various positions.

ATTAINING CULTURAL PLURALISM
AND A MORE HUMANE SOCIETY

Throughout the history of the United States, many have struggled in the pursuit of a just and humane society. They have struggled against hatred, adversity, and indifference, and their battles leave an important legacy in the country's history. In many areas of public policy, we find values in support of justice and equality that exist alongside the expressions of domination and subjugation, and they have been crucial in addressing many forms of inequality. Because of the existence of these contradictions, we believe that there are certain commonly held values that permeate society and exist alongside the oppressive and racist ideology.

For cultural pluralism to exist, a country must permit the cultural differences of its people to exist without punishment or penalty. We believe that the goal of cultural pluralism is a necessary one as the next logical step in the development of a more humane society.

Any effort toward systematic change to eradicate inequality within our society creates fear and repression. Among the critics of cultural pluralism are those who fear that the continuous emergence and proliferation of groups demanding rights and resources will only move our country toward a major upheaval.

In our opinion, these fears do not justify deliberately or unintentionally continuing to subject populations to social and economic disenfranchisement. In order for people from different communities to coexist in a condition of cultural pluralism, members of our society must adhere to certain commonly held values.

The concept of regulative values as formulated by Donald L. Noel states that "regulative values are those values commonly held by members of a society which are generally adhered to through policy positions, social institutions, and other social processes. Priority values that enhance cultural pluralism would include the following: an appreciation for a heterogenous society; appreciation for one's own and others' heritage; appreciation for the unique contributions of each group to our national heritage; appreciation for the value of an individual and his or her historical and cultural context; and a commitment to a society that equitably distributes its resources to all its members."[6]

The models of preferredness and unpreferredness introduce a perspective that allows disenfranchised groups to see their position in relation to others and to those in power. We hope that by recognizing the commonalities of their situations, disenfranchised groups will begin to understand that competition and hostility sustain the existing power base and cause them to miss opportunities for a collective demand for equity and parity on behalf of all citizens. Traditionally cultural pluralism is viewed as a detriment to social harmony, because the recognition of individual cultural groups is perceived as encouraging intrasocietal friction and competition. This view results from the perspective that assimilation, integration, and acculturation are the most desirable goals. Such policy positions are used to support the current arrangements of social, political, and economic inequality. Our task becomes one of projecting the idea that conflict is not a natural condition, but rather the result of values and attitudes that are taught. Disenfranchised groups must learn that it is mutually beneficial to act together to redress their grievances.

To achieve cultural pluralism requires that disenfranchised groups develop a process of validation that emanates from their own history and values. Each group must develop a sense of self that derives from a commonly held belief system, an understanding of the group's historical circumstances, its proven problem-solving processes, and its aspirations for the future. The group must discover, learn about, and document its history as experienced in its nation of origin, and as reflected in the group's experiences in the United States. Group members must hold a vision of the future that reinforces their future viability and existence.

Definitions of individual identity and collective identity must rest on a shared belief system and on a cultural context that is the expression of both aesthetic and material aspects of the group's collective productivity. Serious inquiry into further conceptualization of cultural pluralism as an interdisciplinary concept and as a societal goal raises several questions. We close with the following questions, which we hope will encourage further discussion of pluralism: Are there successful examples of culturally diverse societies where resources and power are collectively shared? Can cultural pluralism exist in different economic and political systems? What comparisons can be made? What relationships, if any, exist between a society's intracultural group relationships and its economic well being, its political leadership, its measure of political liberalism, and its institutionalized religious diversity? What are the next phases in the development of diversified communities? What is the nature of the coalitions that are forming today? What are the goals and objectives of these coalitions? Do these coalitions represent a unification around social class? If so, why have some cultural and ethnic groups transcended class differentiations in their development of strategies for social change? Will the struggle to build a more humane society necessitate violent confrontation? If a confrontation is not imminent, what are the overall relationships, arrangements, and processes necessary for the continuation of a cohesive society?

ENDNOTES

1.   United States Department of Labor, *Workforce 2000: Work and Workers for the 21st Century* (Indiana: Hudson Institute, 1987), p.97.
2.   Horace M. Kallen, *Culture and Democracy in the United States* (New York: Moni and Liveright, 1929), as quoted by Milton M. Gordon in *Assimilation in American Life* (New York: Oxford University Press, 1964) pp. 142-143.
3.   Frank Bonilla, "Cultural Pluralism and the University: The Case of Puerto Rican Studies" (a paper presented at the Seminar on Cultural Pluralism, sponsored by Columbia University and the City College of New York, April 1972).
4.   Antonia Pantoja, Wilhelmina Perry and Barbara Blourock, "Towards the Development of Theory: Cultural Pluralism Redefined," *The Journal of Sociology and Social Work*, vol. 4, no. 1 (September 1976).
5.   Robert Blauner, *Racial Oppression in America* (New York: Harper, 1972), p.67.
6.   Donald L. Noel, "A Theory of the Origin of Ethnic Stratification," *The Journal of Social Problems*, vol. 16, no. 2, Fall, 1968, pp.167-172.

BLACKS IN THE DIASPORA

REDEFINITIONS FOR THE THIRD MILLENNIUM

Rex Nettleford

I listen with interest when a colleague refers to the "reality" of being a "white Cuban" in Miami, of not feeling oppressed, but rather of being part of a majority. Like scores of others, I, too, come from a majority, but that majority is purely numerical. It is a numerical majority that in effect functions as a cultural minority. And by *culture* I mean more than a bit of dance and a bit of music; I refer to the entire universe of cultural indices that cover language, religion, kinship patterns, attitudes to authority and power, modes of production, distribution and exchange, as well as artistic manifestations. An essential understanding of that is necessary for any meaningful discourse. One's concern about oppression cannot be solely with *personal* liberation. All too often, the individual functions within a system that remains dysfunctional for the larger community to which that individual belongs. So, having honors and medals, having even the finest education the mainstream can offer, can amount to little when we consider that there is a much bigger cause out there with which to contend. One is a part of both the problem of, and the solution to, oppression. I have long since gone beyond the provincial concerns of Jamaica, even the wider English-speaking Caribbean, to the reality of the entire

This article was developed from presentations given at the 1989 Cultural Diversity Based on Cultural Grounding Conference and at 1990 follow-up meetings.

Western world.

That present-day reality of that world dates back a half-millennium, if we must put a date on it. There is every reason for Blacks to start thinking in terms of that half-millennium. I use the word *Black* as an umbrella term in the sense that many in the West have used it—to mean non-White, with special reference to persons of African descent. Not that people of African ancestry have a monopoly on oppression over the past 500 years. All people of color have had to carry the burden of a particular kind of oppression in the Americas. The Native Americans, or Amerindians, for example, have been all but exterminated in my part of the world, the Caribbean; the few who survive, whether on the reservations or outside, have been marginalized.

Those of African ancestry, however, were indispensable to the production processes of the Western world. They had to work through the meaning of their experience here. In fact, African Americans have had to carry the responsibility of forging, in the crucible of slavery, throughout plantation America, many of the things that the Latinos are now facing, in freedom, though with the anguish of the "undocumented." Since Blacks are well-schooled in that particular kind of endurance, it makes sense that strategic alliances between the hordes of oppressed should now be formed. The newer arrivals in the U.S. can indeed benefit from the historical experience of the older players in the game, and the older "victims" can be reminded of the existential reality of the newer ones coming in.

It is critical that all of these people work together. This is a major task, however, that will not be completed by tomorrow or in the next decade. The aggrieved and anguished hordes must first engage in the urgent matter of *redefinition*. We have imitated, adapted, and adjusted in the course of our struggles, and now we must *innovate* by destroying the remaining barriers. We cannot afford to indulge in a monodimensional notion of the "oppressed," because that condition does not belong exclusively to any one group. Both the jailor and the jailed are behind bars. One of the things that we have to convey to a Western world intent on dominating what it calls the "lesser races" is that as overseer, it too is in need of liberation.

The liberation for which Blacks, Latinos, and Native Americans are fighting is not the liberation purely of self, but of an entire society, of an entire world. The abolition of the plantation slavery system was not simply the emancipation of the slave, but also the emancipation of the enslaver. The people who have come to the Americas since the abolition of slavery benefitted greatly from these earlier struggles.

I do not think this fundamental contribution by persons of African ancestry is appreciated as much as it should be. In other words, the abolition of slavery was the emancipation, the liberation, of entire societies (and by extension the rest of the Western world). So people who came into the societies of the Americas after slavery was abolished were able to come into societies predicated on individual freedom for all—the core of the American Dream, of British justice, and universal human rights.

After Abolition, some West Indians came in as contract workers, but there were limits defining the extent of their terms of service and of their cultural exclusion. The limits were legally guaranteed and stood defiant of the ambitions of those who would be tempted to maintain the status quo. This was the case with indentured laborers brought in from India and China, the source of much of the new labor supply after West Africa. In fact, each worker carried a *persona* in law and in much else. These were tremendous advances made in terms of human interaction and social relations.

Now, Blacks in the American Diaspora need to consolidate the promise of decency inherited from these struggles, to refine it, and to make it a reality. For this promise is, after all, very much part of the apparatus of historical Black struggle and must continue to be so as part of the serious redefinitions that must be made about the world and about human beings in society, in preparation for the twenty-first century.

That enterprise is already being aided by certain changes in the world at large. The great systems—whether Christianity, capitalism, Islam, or communism—if not bankrupt, have certainly been found wanting. And a great many who have been exposed to these would-be panaceas realize that they are not the total answers for Blacks, who must be careful that in fighting other people's battles, they do not forget their own. I was never myself in favor of joining others in fighting communism, for example, because that was never the battle to be fought by Blacks. Our battle is the one of getting justice for ourselves, and by extension, for all peoples.

How one defines *power* these days is very important. The world still thinks largely in terms of nuclear warheads and other military materiel, though there is ample evidence of the futility and the powerlessness even of those. What is growing stronger is the power of the human spirit. I like to feel that we have to be part of the business of winning the war through the triumph of the human spirit. So, as I said at the conference on cultural diversity in 1989, we have to see power in terms of the empowerment of the human capital. And when one speaks of empowerment, what is one talking about? What does one want power for? If one looks at the groups who now have power, by whatever means one measures that, one finds that they enjoy that status because they are able to define themselves on *their own terms*, they are able to follow through with *action* on the basis of those definitions. I think that what Blacks have to do is aim at the bottom line, whether one defines it in terms of economics, profits, or cultural certitude.

This has serious implications for what is called *multiculturalism*, or that other much abused term, *cultural pluralism*. If you hold the reins, you will be in favor of cultural pluralism because it is the surest way of maintaining the status quo that keeps you in power. In other words, if everybody stays in their own cultural ghettos, those already in control can continue to be decision makers. So here again, the redefinitions and the realignments have got to be the responsibility of Blacks. I don't mean to pretend that we don't live in a society that is culturally complex. We do! But the important thing to stress is that Blacks have been major contributors to that tapestry even though the presumptions of Western civilization place them on the periphery.

A great many things that we consider *American* have been derived from what are called "ethnic minorities," including the struggle for and defense of individual rights. By no means do the Europeans, whether the Pilgrim Fathers or the intellectuals fleeing Hungary, have a monopoly on that contribution. This brings me to that greatest weapon of Black liberation—the mind, the creative intellect. Many Blacks keep referring to the Jews with increasing ambivalence. In the U.S. the influence of the Jews on intellectual culture is often considered way out of proportion to their numbers. If one were to go on Broadway, it would not be unusual to discover that the doorman is a Jew, nor that the theater is also *owned* by a Jew. A few of the top stars in the show, as well as the producer and the director may also be Jewish! There are three key areas in which Jews have concentrated their energies: the arts, media and education, and business. Through these they have tremendous clout in the country's fundamental institutional frameworks. They may not be sitting in the Oval Office, but they may well be exerting influence there by the force of their intellect. It is this concentration of intellect and imagination that has held Western civilization under the spell of Jesus, Marx, Freud, and Einstein—four great shapers of Western thought. One cannot go wrong, then, taking hold of the creative intellect and the creative imagination, coupled with a hold on money.

In the 1980s, former British prime minister Margaret Thatcher's political "love affair" with Ronald Reagan was not just about two conservatives getting together to control market forces. Thatcher felt very strongly that anything "democratic" that the Western world boasts about was given to it by the *Anglo-American* tradition. Such are the tremendous claims made by "cousins" across the North Atlantic, while the 'lesser races' persist with a vengeance in setting the criteria for determining human worth and status among the kith and kin of Western Europeans who have settled in the Americas.

We can virtually all use the public toilets in Atlanta, as they now do in Johannesburg, but that is not only what human dignity is about. There are established cosmologies in Western civilization that are reflected in the way people make decisions, the way they relate to one another, and in the way they build and run their institutions. I think these ideas and customs are in large measure what Blacks are fighting against in the Americas, all over the West, and in South Africa. One therefore has to be very careful not to get trapped in the "melanin syndrome"; being Black or non-White does not mean that a person is any less Eurocentric than the person who is White. It may well be more a matter of culture than of skin.

On the other hand, while White liberal alliance with assertive Blacks is, has always been, and will continue to be critical to the cause, there is a real responsibility on the part of people of non-Caucasian stock to do the job themselves. If they do not assume leadership and take hold of the reins of their own struggle, they will never be able to convince themselves that they can achieve their liberation.

Because of the structure of power in the world over the past half-millennium, those of African ancestry have been the last to enter the game of formal responsibility in the Americas. Everybody else has been ahead or allowed to be ahead in the game. The people of African ancestry, however, have had to survive. They therefore need to focus on the strategies of survival and demarginalization that those in power have devised over the past half-millennium. Today the struggle is even more complex. Blacks have to contend with the Hispanic versus the Anglo struggle on one level. The Latino may be a mestizo with an Amerindian ingredient in some cases. That constitutes yet another dimension of the situation. And the Native American possesses a kind of genealogical pedigree that all but renders everybody else as usurpers of the land.

This is yet another reason why the alliance with the native peoples of the Americas is critical. Mixed-blood Dominicans of Santo Domingo call themselves "Indios"—indicating a clear grasp of the significance of what ancestral pedigree is in the Americas. Whether or not the Amerindians are still alive in the Caribbean and the rest of the Americas, their values and their energy persist. The "usurpers" all learned a great deal from the Amerindian—not just diet, or how to cope with the physical environment, but also the necessary psychic reinforcement for survival on the metaphysical level.

A lot of serious research and analysis of that cultural exchange has to be done, quite frankly, to give to the new peoples of the Americas firmer cultural certitude. The person of European ancestry, though he or she may be totally ignorant, still has the support system of mainstream authority, and on that basis is able to accomplish all sorts of things. The issue of whether White

America considers itself American rather than as Europe Overseas is not always addressed with the candor and courage that is necessary. In the case of the Caribbean and all of Latin America, a "White" Western ethos remains the norm. All of the Americas now have to redefine their reality in defiance of this guiding overlordship. All of the Americas have to "indigenize," and Blacks must be active agents in this enterprise or enter the twenty-first century as the peripheral souls they are still deemed to be. Blacks have to legitimize what they have created out of their historical experience.

The networking modality is vital in this, and the facilitating of such networking is a major task of institutions like the Caribbean Cultural Center. Meanwhile the Latinos, too, as they see necessary, will have to continue fighting their own battles while remaining part of a tapestry. The "melting pot" myth never did seem to make sense anyway; but the notion of a tapestry, in which one can see each thread, with its own color, its own texture, which exists only because the threads are intertwined, suggests an alternative perception. That is another way of looking at the Americas and the modern world, another way of perceiving the product of the last half-millennium of multiple encounters. With the so-called globalization of the planet now, Diaspora Blacks may just have something to offer what presumably will be the challenges of the twenty-first century. With the communications technology revolution, people will be called upon to make sense of the instant chaos with which they are confronted. Humankind will have to learn to see the world in terms of the tapestry I speak of and at the same time be able to identify its threads. Indeed, this is already a way of life with the hustling, resourceful, survival-oriented Africans in the Diaspora.

Still there is a great deal of rethinking, analysis, and reflection that has to be done to inform the practical life lived "out in the sticks," as it were. On a symbolic level, there is absolutely no substitute for Blacks peopling their consciousness with their own as role models. Everyone knows that Blacks can sing and dance; that they can kick and pass a football, box, throw a basketball, and all that. None of those skills should be lost. But there are other things to be done. Blacks will have to be prepared to enter the inner portals of power, such as the finance and business sanctuaries and the arenas of political decision-making, other than the mayoralties of dilapidated inner cities long abandoned by Whites. The success at governance by the largely Black political directorates presiding over the Commonwealth Caribbean, and by the leaders of newly independent states in Africa south of the Sahara, cannot be overemphasized. Blacks will have to help build and reshape the universities, which are important institutions of growth, instruments of development, and key molders of the human mind. And their creative artistic expressions must be liberated from the constraints of being mere "ethnic indulgences." Above all, Blacks must fight such stereotypes every inch of the way.

In the minds of the Establishment in the U.S.A. and the rest of the West, Blacks are considered to be incapable of classicism. Yet the term "classical" has long been associated with the conscious application of the mind to the refinement and internal integration of intellectual and artistic expressions. And although every civilization is by definition capable of this, that capacity is denied to Blacks. They must continue then, to defy such arbitrary categorizations and assert themselves against all efforts to relegate their achievements to the base of the pyramid of human achievement.

The classical expressions in jazz and other forms of American music that are largely rooted in Black traditional and popular lore already attest to this. Today, this genuinely *American* musical form—jazz—is part of the stock and capital of all humanity, as the symphonies, sonatas, concertos and oratorios of Europe have been. A great many Blacks still feel that they must prove to Europe or to Whites at home that they too can do "their thing." That may be fine as tactic and strategy, but it hardly represents the substance of the struggle for liberation.

The fact that there are Blacks performing European classical ballet does not say all there is to say about the art of dance. Nor does the existence of Black divas and Black symphony conductors necessarily advance the art of music in any seminal sense. Art forms that draw energy from the tabernacles of the American South or from the vodun temples, shango rituals, and kumina ceremonies of the Caribbean are bound to be of greater significance in the long run. The twenty-first century, in assessing the achievement of twentieth-century contributions to the advancement of civilization—whether in science, the arts, or the humanities—will have to pay attention to these true originals.

Leontyne Price, to her credit, admits to feeling at home when she sings Black spirituals, despite her royal triumphs on the opera stage. But America's Ella Fitzgerald and Aretha Franklin are also among the century's great classical musical artists. Even in the matter of the arts, where Blacks already excel, a great deal of redefining and reassessment has to be done. Surely White scholars who go to the ghetto or the reservation in search of anthropological specimens realize that White suburban America has its anthropology as well, although those studies are likely to be labeled otherwise in the finely crafted lexicography of racism.

A major responsibility for Diaspora Blacks is to help change people's attitudes to the diversity of humankind's creative imagination. In order to do so Blacks must begin with themselves. They are among the greatest purveyors of myths about themselves. What happens in South Africa is understandably of tremendous interest to the Diaspora. What happens in the United States of America and in England is no less so! Recent events in France, where a law against anti-Semitism in politics had to be passed, are of interest not only to Jewish people. The Jews have cemeteries and other forms of property that have been desecrated, but Blacks have been having much trouble in France as well. What is interesting is that it was an anti-Jewish event that precipitated that legislation.

In the time of Josephine Baker, France was supposed to be a psychic haven for Black people. But then again, to many French folks the undoubtedly remarkable Miss Baker was a nice showgirl—chocolate brown, leggy, and exotic. Again, the old stereotypes! She of course did what she had to do, and grew famous as a result. Blacks have to let the rest of the world know that they are not there simply to titillate the appetites of tired businessmen. That fact was not lost on the indefatigable freedom fighter that Ms. Baker turned out to be.

Interestingly enough, notions of Black inferiority were not part of human thinking before this fateful half-millennium. It is over that protracted period of imperialism and trans-Atlantic slavery and the tremendous success of these aberrations, that humankind was able to develop and hone this obscenity of institutionalized racism as part of the so-called triumph of the West.

Now, at the end of the century, there seems to be a mood for change. One of the good things about all this is that the West is itself somewhat confused at the moment. Europe is uniting, but Japan, once considered the "Yellow Peril" in the West, is not weakening economically. The United States is seriously in debt even as it ascends to the position of sole, though fragile, Superpower, now that the Soviet Union has disintegrated. One should not have been surprised at what happened in Eastern Europe beginning in 1989, though change came so rapidly. The sluggishness with which the pillars of apartheid are being dismantled in South Africa stands out in sharp contrast. There, as elsewhere, power is still regarded as best left in the hands of the civilized. And being "civilized" still carries the old-fashioned stamp of a particular skin color and cultural pedigree that the country's Black majority supposedly does not possess.

Moreover, with the collapse of communism, Europe now has its own Third World. Aid is now directed to kith and kin across the North Atlantic, and from London, Paris, and Bonn to Prague, Budapest, and Warsaw. It is important that Blacks in the Diaspora understand the nature of such phenomena. And as I said before, the imperative of finding new paradigms not only for Blacks themselves but also for the wider world, must be high on the agenda of Black development.

Blacks have always known that social interaction and human interdependence are inescapable facts of life. The powerful North Atlantic nations, on the other hand, collectively continue to indulge the myth that a dependent South needs the prosperous North more than the North needs the South. Blacks throughout the Americas realize that if they did not exist, they would have had to be invented, if only for the kind of encounters that have served to give the Americas their strengths and weaknesses, their vulnerability and their resilience. So, contrary to established beliefs—from the notion of Iberian discovery to the current claims of Whites to scientific and technological superiority—Blacks in the Diaspora have been integrally part of the process leading to all that constitutes the contemporary Americas.

GHOSTS

Peter H. Pennekamp

The question before this panel is whether Western European culturally specific institutions are obsolete. It is an odd question. Under our continental/cultural concepts of Europe, Africa, the Americas, Asia, or Australia, we manage to homogenize vast spectrums of cultures. The question asked is undoubtedly not concerned with the cultural halls of Irish, Scot, Lithuanian, or Portuguese immigrants. It is not about Appalshop in Whitesburg, Kentucky, the Helena Film Society in Montana, or, I would guess, even the 92nd Street Y in New York City. The question intended is whether the large historically white institutions operating under *broad public mandate* are now obsolete. There is an important distinction to be made here. A simplistic, monolithic view of Europe—or Eurocentrism—leads to endless misunderstandings. To answer the question posed requires a better sense of what we are talking about, of why these institutions assume authority, and of historical context, which I think of as listening to ghosts.

I spend a fair amount of time in big cultural institutions listening to the moan and clank of ghosts. I listen to the clatter and the silences of the particular building. The ghosts tell more about the place than fancy brochures, or annual reports. The anxious whisperings of dedicated curators and programmers committed to their chosen fields are omnipresent, yet other ghosts whisper of tottering monarchy, of authority fearful because of its weakening hold. Present are the ghosts of class and racial exclusion, who say "yes, these places are public, but despite all rhetoric to the contrary, only for the *right* public."

This article is based on remarks delivered on October 18, 1991, at the Cultural Diversity Based on Cultural Grounding II Conference held in New York City.

The United States confronts the twenty-first century with no "right" public remaining, but with a varied public to serve. Institutions will demonstrate whether or not they are obsolete by the way they respond to this heterogeneous nation. Historically, the power of the big institutions comes from an assumption of the cultural ascendancy of the West that looks backward to the nineteenth century, not forward to the twenty-first. It's a popular, highly romanticized, and inaccurate concept of the West's history.

If one looks at the historical id, not the ego, of Europe in the period leading up to the "Age of Exploration," certainly one finds it to be messy, violent, and "barbaric." Europe of the thirteenth, fourteenth, and fifteenth centuries was hardly a desirable place. It was riddled with pestilence, ground down by abuses of feudal power, trampled by invasion, and torn by religious conflict. Especially those who were at the top of the economic and political hierarchy were looking to extend their grasp of resources. The powerful classes, and often the church, had a tremendous drive to "exploit" new lands and resources. This usually led them to each other's throats, resulting in endless wars that devastated the countryside. During the period when the Americas were charted, the poor often had serious reason to leave Europe if the opportunity presented itself.

The Spanish Inquisition was in full bloom in 1492 when Columbus set sail. In the fifteen years prior to the grand inquisitor Torquemada's retirement in 1496, some 2,000 "heretics" were executed by church officials. In 1492, all Jews and Muslims in Spain were given the choice of converting to Christianity, leaving Spain, or being condemned by the Inquisition. Later, the Reformation did its own fair share of religious murder. When Europeans traveled to other parts of the world and discovered what they classified as "barbaric" practices, they must have felt right at home.

In her book, *A Distant Mirror,* Barbara Tuchman describes a thirteenth-century army plundering across Western Europe, destroying people, livestock, and foodstuffs until, in winter, virtually the entire army starved to death. Conditions in Europe were made worse by the bubonic plague, which killed an estimated one-quarter of all Europeans in the fourteenth century. There were repeated plague outbreaks between then and 1603, when the "great epidemic" swept England. Between 1603 and 1665, 150,000 people died in London alone.

Events in England around and after 1492 give us a sense of the place that rank-and-file colonists were leaving. It was a tough place to live. Columbus sailed only thirty-nine years after the Hundred Years War ended and seven years after the War of the Roses. Conflict among Catholic church, king, and Protestantism set the stage for the 1500s, when England continuously bent its will against Scotland and Wales, seeking to subjugate them under a "united" rule. In 1642 the country was torn by civil war. Charles I was beheaded in 1649. A revolution in 1688 sent King James II fleeing to France. In 1702 England was drawn into the War of Spanish Secession. In 1707 Scotland and Wales were finally annexed, and Great Britain was created. During 1745 and 1746, the Scots rebelled under Bonnie Prince Charlie. Upon the Scots' defeat, the English killed the major clan chiefs, disarmed Scotland, and banned kilts and bagpipes. (This year, in 1992, the majority of Scots once again expressed, through the ballot, their wish for secession from England.) England went to war with France in 1756, and in the colonies this was known as the French and Indian War.

English colonists came here under trying circumstances, not as bearers of a particularly advanced culture. According to sociologist Stephen Steinberg, author of *The Ethnic Myth,* as many as 30,000 English and 7,500 Irish homeless and convicted were sent to the colonies. Between 1750 and 1770, some 20,000 convicts were sent to Maryland alone. The author Samuel Johnson called Americans a "race of convicts." One-half to two-thirds of whites who came to the colonies did so as indentured servants, having received transport in exchange for seven years of labor that amounted to slavery. Any colonists had little to lose and much to gain in risking war with the Indian nations in an attempt to find a better place for themselves.

The negative aspects of European history are generally forgotten when England and Western Europe are hailed for bringing civilization to these and other shores. The great cultural expressions of Europe are important but there is no particular historical reason to believe that they are a civilized force. They are joined in this land by the massive accomplishments of other continents (including this one!) that have contributed to America's unique culture. It is in our mix that we are strong—not in illusions of a singular core cultural origin.

Furthermore, within the broad European cultural region, there were and are many cultural frameworks. The European cultural hegemony that we call *Eurocentricity* does not include most of the creative forces of Europe. It is limited to a narrow range of culture defined by patrons, royalty, academics, and the financially privileged. Within that narrow range exist many wonderful expressive beliefs and practices. When we talk about Eurocentrism, however, we are actually leaving out most Europeans.

Europe itself is a more or less contemporary concept. As recently as the early part of this century, Europeans were classified by nationality, and nationality was often considered "race." Irish were considered a different race than Italians, each with special racial characteristics. This was readily accepted by most Americans.

With the subjugation of the Indian nations in North America, the Anglo-Saxon population of the U.S. dominated the country until the great European immigrations of the nineteenth century. At that time Anglo-Saxon Americans were fairly overrun by the influx of largely working-class or peasant Jews, Slavs, Irish, and others who were coming in unprecedented numbers to the United States. As documented by cultural historian Lawrence Levine, educational theorist Graeme Chalmers, and others, scientists of the time went to extremes to justify the prevailing social and class order by demonstrating that these immigrants were racially inferior. The Irish, for example, faced much of the same sort of prejudice that African Americans continue to face today. Derogatory "scientific" claims were believed broadly by Anglo-Saxon Americans, ironically called "Native Americans" at the time, well into the early part of this century. Anglo-Saxon America responded to that earlier European "threat" of cultural diversity by creating social barriers. If there was no way to keep *those* people out (and besides, their labor was needed in sweat shops, on railroads, and in the mines), one didn't have to associate with them. From private clubs to college and university entrance requirements, the country was made safe for class and racial separation.

If art is an expression of a culture's most deeply held values, it is not surprising that among the efforts at social exclusion were the building of cultural institutions often inhospitable to the fabled "huddled masses." The Anglo-Saxon "natives" who ran the country built these institutions to represent the cultural standards for all Americans to follow if they were to be accepted by the genteel classes. The huddled masses weren't supposed to attend the opera, symphony, theater, or visit the museums, at least not until they had come out of the melting pot into proper society.

It's hard for many of us who are cultural workers to come to grips with the way in which many major cultural institutions continue to assume an exclusive role, while advancing art that is often wonderful. We have difficulty accepting the role these institutions have played in separating the art from a large public and conversely excluding much of American artistry from "public" culture.

When I listen to the ghosts of publicly mandated institutions, I hear a babble. The babble is of confusion and of institutional uncertainty. In the face of a changing mandate, institutions that dominate resources, yet hold a narrow point of view, vaccilate. There is a sadness in this. The music of Mozart, who loved to see his work popularized, may become the victim of the exclusivity of the contemporary orchestra.

We forget that institutions don't really exist in and of themselves. When the people are gone and the wind comes through and blows away the printed programs, the debris of class, racism, and assumed ascendancy, what's left are just hollow caverns. They must be adapted by human beings and spirited in new ways if they are to be vital contributors to our society.

FROM CALIFORNIA TO NOVA HISPANIA

REFLECTIONS ON THE CULTURAL DEBATES

Guillermo Gómez-Peña

Like many of you, I wear many hats as a bilingual poet, an artist-activist, and an intercultural diplomat—in my case, without official representation. I feel like I can best contribute to this dialogue by sharing with you some poems, memories, and political ideas. I wish to establish some links between the Columbian legacy and the present situation of our communities and our institutions. Please bear with my disnarrative thinking.

Mexican and, therefore, Chicano culture, since the much touted discovery, and more recently since the 1848 transfer of territory, has been the result of an ongoing clash of disparate cultures, languages, artistic and spiritual traditions, and political systems. And we have learned to live within this syncretism, within the ever-clashing waves that frame our experience. As Mexicans we are crucified by the North, the South, the East, and the West. We are Indios, Mestizos, and Spanish, therefore, also, Arabic. Many of our *paisanos* have African, French, and Jewish blood, and since the fifties—today more than ever—U.S. pop culture has penetrated every aspect of our lives via television, tourism, rock 'n' roll, fashion, and food. Though the Other is always inside of us, Anglo-

This text was excerpted from various essays and performance texts created by the author and presented as the keynote address of the panel "Are Western European Culturally Specific Institutions Obsolete?" at the Cultural Diversity Based on Cultural Grounding II Conference on October 18, 1991, in New York City.

American culture has managed to make us a double Other—within and outside. I hope with my work to function as a mirror between the two, the North in the South, the South in the North, and us in between.

> *One night I was beaten up by a biker gang from Hollywood*
> *one of my first leading roles in an American thriller*
> *they mistook me for a Columbian dealer*
> *a Filipino boxer, a Libyan pachuco*
> *a Hawaiian surfer*
> *who knows what they thought they knew?*
> *I've been mistaken so many times in America*
> *but then who hasn't been?*
> *People here tend to mistake one another's identities*
> *It's like a national sport.*
> *Are you Peruvian or Venezuelan?*
> *Were you speaking Mexican or Spanish?*
> *Did I see you on TV last night?*
> *Did I see you on the TV of my fears?*

> *When Columbus arrived on La Hispaniola*
> *he was convinced he had found a shortcut to the Indies.*
> *The very discovery of this continent was a flat*
> *   misunderstanding*
> *and let's not forget that misunderstanding*
> *is the seed of all violence*
> *When President Bush arrived in Saudi Arabia*
> *he was convinced he had found a shortcut*
> *to the New World Order*
> *but his interpretation of Islam was a flat misunderstanding*
> *and let's not forget that misunderstanding*
> *is the seed of all violence.*

We're living inexplicable contradictions that shatter our understanding of the world. As the Soviet Union and Eastern Europe welcome structural changes, the U.S. power structure

withdraws into its old Republican model. As Latin America finally gets rid of its last military dictators, the U.S. becomes more
heavily militarized. While diplomatic negotiation and intercultural
dialogue emerge as viable options to construct a peaceful future—
haven't we seen enough examples of transition without rupture in
other countries?—the United Nations begins to practice panic politics in the Middle East. While other civilian societies are being
led by Utopian reformists, such as Mandela, Aristide, and Havel,
we're being misled by hemispheric machos. While artists and writers in other countries are leading the way to the next century, we're
being cut back, censored, and excluded from the political process.
We face a strange historical dilemma. We stand equidistant from
Utopia and Armageddon, with one foot on each side of the border.
And our art and thought reflect this condition.

> *"There is a distance between us*
> *that reminds me of who I am*
> *nehuatl nimopo*
> *nehuatl oic onimitzcocolli"*
> *says Cuauhtemoc to Cortes while being tortured*
> *Mas lo cortes no quita lo culero*
> *Spanish Lesson #1:*
> *Culero es aquel*
> *que conociendo dos o mas lenguajes*
> *solo te muestra uno.*
> *Translation:*
> *Culeirou is someone who speaks*
> *two or more languages,*
> *but always answers in the one you don't know.*
> *Bush tambien es un culeirou*
> *Blackout!*

In the 1980s, an increased awareness of the existence and
importance of multicentric perspectives and hybrid cultures within the U.S. made us rethink the implications of otherness. With
demographic shifts, generalized political turmoil, global media,
and the exposure to non-Anglo-European art and thought, leading
to intensified traffic between North and South and East and West,

ethnocentric notions of "Western culture" toppled by their own weight. Latin America and Asia are already entrenched in North America, Africa slowly moves North into Europe, and after a four-decade long ideological divorce, Eastern and Western Europe are intermingling again. In this moving cartography, it becomes increasingly harder to sustain essentialist positions. Multilingualisms, syncretic aesthetics, and cultural pluralism have been common practices on this continent. And not because of matters of status or fashion. But because of a basic political necessity. To study the history, art, and political thought of our neighboring Others, and to learn other languages becomes indispensible if we want to cross borders, reclaim our American continent, and participate in the drafting of the next century's cartography.

The holders of the political, economic, and cultural power, including the broadcasting systems that shape and define our notions of the world, act extremely scared of these changes. Unable to comprehend their place and role in this still incomprehensible cartography, they feel that the world and the future are no longer theirs, and they anxiously want them back. Their fears have reached neurotic proportions, and their response has been far from enlightened. They are currently doing everything they can to control the entry of the Other and to reconquer the not-so-New World, a territory that they feel by historical and cultural right belongs only to them.

> *Five centuries*
> *four races*
> *three languages*
> *two faces*
> *one heart*
> *Action!*
> *The night before the awaited arrival*
> *the Admiral of the Ocean Sea*
> *confronts his restless crew*
> *"no se asusten carnales*
> *It's only me,*
> *The trans-Atlantic vato*
> *I've got some questions for you*

Are you a citizen of this time and place
or are you still clinging to a dying order?
Are you willing to dialogue?
or are you going to shoot me after the show?
Are you ready to co-write with me the next chapter?"

Matachin
remember only what you want
The rest is poisonous algae
toxic waste in your mental tundra
linguo lae ars fronterica

Tenochtitlan, 1512.
Spanish becomes the official language
of Nova Hispania
San Diego, 1988.
English becomes the official language of the Southwest.

In many ways, multiculturalism went sour. We managed to turn the continent upside down, so to speak, and insert the discourse and the terminology, and turn attention toward non-Anglo-European experimental artists in the central platform of discussion. We even managed to alter the funding criteria a bit. But we weren't able to reform the administrative structure of the national institutions. They remain largely monocultural. Today, many talk about how exciting, necessary, confusing, or exclusionary multiculturalism is. Responses range from willingness to fund and promote this cause to militant anger at the prospect of sharing money and notoriety with artists from other ethnic backgrounds, to fighting about whose suffering deserves more attention.

The debate has already reached the mainstream, yet the crucial political issues are still being avoided. Blockbuster exhibits present "multicultural art" as the "cutting edge," yet, with a few exceptions, there is no mention of the historical crimes and social inequities that lie beneath the neocolonial relationship between Anglo-European culture and its Others. Like the United Colors of Benetton ads, a Utopian discourse of sameness helps to erase all unpleasant stories. The message is a refried colonial idea. If we merely hold hands and dance mambo together, we can effectively abolish ideology, sexual and cultural politics, and class differences.

Let's face it, the missing text is very sad. In 1991, racism, xenophobia, and ethnocentrism are alive and well in the United States of America. And the communities that reflect more proportionately the multicultural composition of society are the homeless, the prisoners, persons with AIDS, and the soldiers who came back from the Persian Gulf.

The word *multicultural* hasn't even been properly defined. Due to the lack of an accumulative memory that codifies public debate in America, it seems that every year we have to start the discussion from zero, and therefore we still can't agree on a basic definition. What are the differences between the multi-, inter-, intra-, and crosscultural? What do we exactly mean by cultural equity, diversity, and pluralism? What are the differences between coexistence, exchange, dialogue, collaboration, fusion, hybridization, appropriation, and creative expropriation. These terms are very different. Some overlap and others even have opposite meanings. We often use them indistinguishably, however. As philosophers, practitioners, or impresarios, we must ask some key questions. Which of these forms of relationships between cultures are more symmetrical and desirable, and which are more reactionary. Which are the ones that truly empower us, which ones are new names for old ideas, and which ones are new realities in search of a better name. Where exactly do we stand?

The enigmatic unwillingness of some artists and "minority" (I hate that word) organizations to participate in the debate is a matter of economics. We know that if we blindly join in, the larger organizations that have more connections and credibility, and better grant writers, will intercept the funding and function as multicultural metasponsors. "It shouldn't come as no surprise [sic] that fear exists within third world organizations," writes cultural critic Coco Fusco, "that the current multicultural impetus will ultimately hurt, not help them." If the term *multiculturalism* really meant cultural democracy and institutional collaboration, I am sure that these problems wouldn't exist, and by now we would be in a much more advanced stage of the process.

We must watch out. The multicultural debate hasn't even engendered significant change, and there is already a backlash. Many Anglo-Americans who have been unable to find a place at the multicultural dinner table are becoming increasingly more vocal against racial, sexual, and political difference. The far right is lumping all politicized matters of otherness under the label of "political correctness" and branding it the new intellectual tyranny. After 500 years of systematic exclusion and indifference, they don't want to give us a few more years of attention. If we don't act fast and restore clarity and dignity to the debate, soon we might lose the little territory we so painfully gained in the past five years. The impulse behind this confusing debate is the collective realization that we need to readjust our anachronistic national institutions and policies to the new social, cultural, linguistic, and demographic realities of the country.

What we all are clumsily trying to say in this country is that we want to be part of a *multi*participatory society, one that truly embraces us all, including the multiracial and multisexual communities, the hybrids, the recent immigrants from the South and the East, the children and elderly people, our most vulnerable and beloved ones, the persons with AIDS, and the homeless, whose only mistake is not being able to afford housing. This is not radical politics, but elemental humanism. From rap music to performance art, and from neighborhood politics to the international forums, our contemporary culture is already reflecting this quest.

> *The Spaniards arrived on a Monday.*
> *I left my country on a Tuesday.*
> *The San Juanico Fire occurred on a Wednesday*
> *and the Mexico City Earthquake on a Thursday.*
> *My father died on a Friday.*
> *My son was born on a Saturday.*
> *And my worst performance ever*
> *took place on a Sunday, I think.*

In each of these days
a bunch of us Mexican wolves
got together to lick each other's tears,
'cause you know, carnales,
this kind of pain is only bearable as ritual.
And my psyche is the only document left
a performance document
for the end-of-century society.
Recordamos. We remember. We remember.

We remember dreaming about the arrival of Cortes
not knowing exactly what a hairy man on a horse was.
We thought the Spaniards were gods
and our fate was to welcome them.
We still carry the weight of that mistake.
We also remember the arrival of the first turista,
not knowing exactly
what a blond man on a donkey was.
We thought the gabachos were gods
and our fate was to welcome them.
Ladies and gentlemen,
it is my fate to welcome you
to my performance continent.

Just to finish. My generation was born and raised in a world of multiple crises and continuing fragmentation. Our lives now are framed by the sinister Bermuda Triangle of war, AIDS, and recession. We seem to be closer than ever to the end, and precisely because of this, our actions have twice as much meaning and moral weight, though perhaps less resonance. Our fragile contemporaries are starving, migrating, and dying at very young ages. And the art we are making already reflects this sense of emergency. But it is not enough to just make art. We must step outside of the safe art arena and attempt to recapture our stolen political will and mutilated civilian selves. As the 1990s unfold, U.S. artists, cultural organizers, and intellectuals must perform central roles in the making of a society beyond Columbus. We must fine tune our multiple roles as intercultural diplomats, border philosophers, alternative chroniclers, and activists for world glasnost and local *Gringostroika*. We must practice, promote, and demand access, tolerance, dialogue, and reform. We must defend the survival of the art world as a demilitarized zone. We must continue to support the community centers and the alternative spaces, the last bastions of political and cultural freedom, which are potentially facing extinction. The large institutions must try to keep the smaller ones from sinking, for without them the large institutions would lose their roots and their seeds. We must listen carefully to other cultures who have a long history of facing repression, censorship, and exclusion. Native Americans, Latinos, African Americans, and Asian Americans have been fighting these battles for centuries.

We must rebuild community through our art, for our communities have been dismembered. The insidious colonial tendencies we have internalized and that express themselves in sadistic competition for money, political cannibalism, and moral distrust must be overcome. We must realize we are not one another's enemies and that the true enemy is currently enjoying our divisiveness. We must dialogue and collaborate with artists from other disciplines and ethnic communities, as well as with political activists, educators, lawyers, journalists, cultural critics, and social scientists. The old schism between artists and academics must be resolved once and for all. We must come to the realization that we both have been equally marginalized and that, therefore, we need one another. Artists need the intellectual rigor of academics, and they need our skills to popularize issues. They have access to more extensive information, and we have access to more diverse audiences. Together we can develop a national consensus of priorities and strategies for the new decade.

The survival of the human species is a concern to all communities. Some people say that the 1990s will be the decade of the environment, and I wish with all my heart they were right. But, as performance artist Ellen Sebastian says, "We, the human beings, are the ultimate environment." From Sao Paulo to Baghdad and from Soweto to the Bronx, we are a fauna in danger of extinction. Our ecosystems, the deteriorated multiracial cities we inhabit, are part of the nature we must save. If we don't save the human being and his and her concentrated habitat, we won't even be here to witness the extinction of the great whale or the California condor.

I remember falling into a trance on a stage.
I remember the day I came back from the flower wars.
Ixtaccihuatl had turned into ice for me.
I had decided to let myself die,
to fulfill the damned prophecy,
but instead, I parted.
Left my skin without color
and crossed the border of Anahuac
to regain the desired citizenship
they had so cruelly denied me.

But meanwhile,
at the new Taco Bell of San Juan Capistrano,
undocumented Christopher Columbus
tired, ill & misunderstood
scribbles a strange letter to Queen Isabella.
Salve Reina de todos los Imperios.
My phony green card states
Resident Alien 00141932
My last medical exams reveal
high cholesterol and low blood pressure.
My bank account is empty,
my desire is one day to go back
from California to Nova Hispania
and further back
from Salvador Island to Palos
My ergo motto reads:
to sail the waves of Horror Vacui
Will you wait for me
on the other side of the Ocean?
Will you wait for me
on the other side of my tongue?
Will my voice break into your future dreams,
or will you be dead when I go back?

APPENDIX

CULTURAL DIVERSITY BASED ON CULTURAL GROUNDING II

Ratification Statement
October 19, 1991

The following are the consolidated recommendations of the general body, which we present for your ratification. Ratification means that we agree on the stated goal or objective and are willing to carry forward the work necessary to complete the goal or objective.

(1) It is the consensus of the general body that we need a formalized network to facilitate interchange between our various communities, and between individuals and organizations within our communities.
We further believe that this network should work for the cultural empowerment of our communities. This network must not only speak to information-sharing, but also to advocacy and social action on behalf of our goal of community cultural empowerment.

[We call for ratification of a network. Do we have agreement? Are there any objections?]
[Ratified and Accepted.]

(2) It is the consensus of the general body that the leadership
of this network be chosen from this body.
We propose to begin with the facilitators of each group
working collectively to elect our leadership and that the
facilitators meet following this general session to formal-
ize their leadership.

[We call for ratification of the group facilitators as the initial
leadership of our network.]
[Agreed.]

(3) The general body had specific concerns, which they directed this network and its leadership to address. We list
these concerns:

a. OBJECTIVES That in all levels of activity we remain
conscious of the need to keep our work grounded in community practice, that we not only build coalitions across
cultural borders, but also among traditionally disenfranchised and oppressed peoples.
That further, we actively seek out and encourage cross-
cultural projects that are designed to address empowering
our communities and the culture of our communities,
rather than concentrating on inclusion in or opposition to
dominant-culture Eurocentric institutions and cultural
expressions.
That we actively seek out and work with like-minded
individuals and organizations that are grounded in their
respective communities and that have a history of practice in the expressions or presentation of community-ori-
ented culture.
That the network seek always to encourage both local
empowerment and international exchange.

b. SPECIFIC CONCERNS That a newsletter promote our
objectives by listing names and contact information of all
the founding member individuals and institutions. That
the newsletter include a map and that copies of the

newsletter be made available for dissemination at the local level.

That further, this publication should begin to critically address issues confronting our cultural communities, such as:

   i. Interaction with and utilization of the mass media, both print and electronic

   ii. Exchange of information about activities of member groups

   iii. Documentation and case studies of community struggles for cultural empowerment

   iv. Development and sharing of techniques for dealing with funding agencies (both tax-based public agencies and private philanthropic agencies).

We call for the ratification of these specific recommendations to be addressed through our network newsletter and through other means of data gathering and information exchange that might be developed in the future.
[Agreed.]

(4) There is a need for a unified language and definition of terms that we can all use as a common tongue to define our realities and clearly state our aspirations.
We call for the development of such a lexicon and the discussion of the lexicon within the network.
We call for the ratification of this charge to our leadership.
[Agreed.]

(5) The consensus of the general body is that we stress the need for a work style that is inclusive and democratic and that is representative of community-based cultural expressions.
Toward that end we encourage each member to focus on identifying and working with community individuals and organizations, especially to include those who are outside of the formal network of organizations and individuals who seek grants.

We encourage each member to be active in debates on public policy on the redistribution of funds and resources for cultural activity in their community.
To also seek alternative means of economic development. That network communities initiate local activities consistent with our goals and objectives of cross-cultural networking and community empowerment.

[We call for the ratification of this work style.]
[Agreed.]

(6) Finally, the consensus is that we continue this struggle here and now.
We call for all who agree to join our network, here and now to write down and leave their name and contact information. Further, we call for each person who is able to pay the annual membership dues of $25 here and now.

[We call for ratification of this struggle in the here and now.]
[Agreed.]

CONTRIBUTORS

DR. MOLEFI KETE ASANTE is a professor and chairman of the department of African American Studies at Temple University in Philadelphia. He is the founder of the Afrocentric school of thought. His books include *Afrocentricity* and *Kemet, Afrocentricity and Knowledge.*

DAVID BRYAN is director of Onyx Consultancy in London, which provides arts research, management, and development services. He has been an arts administrator on the local, regional, and national levels in England and led the development of London's largest Black arts center, Brixton Village, in the mid-1980s.

DUDLEY COCKE is the director of Roadside Theater, a part of the collective, Appalshop, which has been making films, videotapes, records, plays, radio programs, and photographs about Appalachia for the past 22 years. Roadside Theater is an ensemble company creating original plays celebrating and examining the region's culture and history. The work of both Roadside and Appalshop is seen nationally and internationally. Cocke, who lives in Whitesburg, Kentucky, is a director, playwright, and producer. He often speaks and writes about rural cultural issues.

HAROLD CRUSE is emeritus professor of history and Afro-American studies at the University of Michigan. He is the author of *The Crisis of the Negro Intellectual, Rebellion or Revolution?* and *Plural but Equal: Blacks and Minorities in America's Plural Society.*

GUILLERMO GOMEZ-PENA was born and raised in Mexico City. He is an interdisciplinary artist and writer who has been exploring cross-cultural issues and North-South relations through performance, radio art, book art, bilingual poetry, journalism, video, and installation art. His essays have been instrumental in the development of the debates on cultural identity. He lives in California. In 1991 he was awarded a MacArthur Fellowship.

GAWANAHS, TONYA GONNELLA FRICHNER is an activist and attorney who is founder and president of the American Indian Law Alliance in New York City, an organization that focuses on legal issues affecting Indian survival. She serves on the advisory committee to the United Nations for the 1993 International Year of the World's Indigenous Peoples.

CHERYLL Y. GREENE (co-editor) heads Cheryll Y. Greene Editorial Services in New York City, which specializes in book development projects. She has worked closely with some of America's finest authors, journalists, and scholars for over twenty years. Her current client list includes major authors, publishers, and cultural institutions, among them the Schomburg Center for Research in Black Culture, Amistad Press, Inc., and Blackside, Inc., producers of the renowned television series, *Eyes on the Prize.* Her forthcoming edited work is *Malcolm X: Make it Plain,* for Blackside, Inc. (Viking), based on the upcoming film to be broadcast on public television in 1994.

G. PETER JEMISON is director of the Ganondagan State Historic Site in Victor, New York, and also a painter whose work has been exhibited nationally.

MARGO MACHIDA is an artist, independent curator, and writer who specializes in contemporary Asian American visual art. For the Asia Society Galleries, she is currently curating a traveling exhibition of first-generation Asian-born artists in America, dealing with issues of cross-cultural identity, which is scheduled to open in 1994.

AMALIA MESA-BAINS is an independent artist and cultural critic. Her artworks, primarily interpretations of traditional Chicano altars, resonate both in contemporary formal terms and in their ties to her Chicano community and history. She is an author of scholarly articles and a nationally known lecturer on Latino art. Throughout her crossdisciplinary career, she has worked to define a Chicano and Latino aesthetic in the U.S. and in Latin America. She lives in San Francisco and is currently involved in multicultural educational research at Far-West Laboratories.

REX NETTLEFORD a former Rhodes Scholar, is professor of continuing studies and a pro vice-chancellor at the University of the West Indies at Mona, Jamaica. A leading Caribbean intellectual, author, and creative artist, Professor Nettleford is also founder, artistic director, and principal choreographer of the internationally acclaimed National Dance Theatre Company of Jamaica.

ANTONIA PANTOJA, Ph.D. is an educator and a community-development activist. She has spent her life building institutions, primarily with her own Puerto Rican community in the United States. The other part of her professional life has been spent as an educator in traditional and nontraditional institutions of higher education. Dr. Pantoja has been the founder of a large number of Puerto Rican institutions in the U.S., among them ASPIRA, Boricua College, and the Puerto Rico Forum. She lives in Puerto Rico, where she is a cofounder of PRODUCIR, Inc., one of the first economic development corporations there.

PETER H. PENNEKAMP is executive director of the Humboldt Area Foundation in Bayside, California, which assists community nonprofit agencies. He is formerly a vice-president of National Public Radio's Cultural Programming and Program Services division. He has devoted a great deal of his career to promoting the cultural pluralism that is central to the contemporary American experience.

WILHELMINA PERRY, Ph.D. is an educator with extensive administrative and teaching experience at both the university and community levels. She is an activist with many years of experience in the areas of institution building, community action research, and community economic development. Her work has centered on disenfranchised communities, especially her own African American one. She lives in Puerto Rico and is a cofounder of PRODUCIR, Inc.

BERNICE JOHNSON REAGON, a curator in the Division of Community Life at the Smithsonian Institution, National Museum of American History, is a specialist in African American oral, performance, and protest traditions. During the Civil Rights Movement, she was a member of the original SNCC (Student Non-Violent Coordinating Committee) Freedom Singers. She founded and currently serves as artistic director of Sweet Honey in the Rock, an internationally acclaimed African American women a cappella quintet. In 1989 she received a MacArthur Fellowship award.

KALAMU YA SALAAM is a New Orleans-based writer and music producer.

ESI SUTHERLAND-ADDY is a research fellow in African languages and literature at the Institute of African Studies at the University of Ghana. She was founding chairperson of the management committee of the W.E.B. DuBois Memorial Centre for Pan African Culture in Accra. Since 1986 she has served in the national government as Deputy Minister for Education in Charge of Higher Education and is at the forefront of educational reform programs in Ghana.

JOHN KUO WEI TCHEN is a cultural activist and a historian. He is the director of the Asian/American Center and a professor of urban studies at Queens College of the City University of New York. He is cofounder of the Chinatown History Museum (New York Chinatown History Project). He speaks and writes regularly on museums, cultural studies, race relations, and American culture.

MARTA MORENO VEGA (co-editor) is executive director of the
Franklin H. Williams Caribbean Cultural Center African Diaspora
Institute, one of New York City's leading cultural institutions,
which she founded in 1976. She helped create two other vital insti-
tutions in the 1970s, El Museo del Barrio and the Association of
Hispanic Arts. She is currently a doctoral candidate at Temple
University.

INDEX

Academia of La Nueva Raza, 50

Acevedo, Mario, 55

African American cultural empowerment, 119, 121, 123, 125,
127, 129, 131, 133, 135, 137,
139, 141, 143

African Diaspora, 12, 14, 17-18

Afro-Americans, 135

AIDS, 170-172

Alcatraz, 50

All-Indian Pueblo Council, 50

Alurista, 41, 48, 55-59, 61, 63-64, 66

Amazon, 64

American Blacks, 15, 151

American Diaspora, 151

Amerindians, 65, 150, 154

Ancient Egypt, 14

Anglican, 96-97

Aranda, Guillermo, 55

Arawaks, 105

Arte Chicano, 66

Asian Americans, 8, 23, 85-86, 88,
173; Asian American Art
Network, 85; Asian Cultural
Council, 86

Association of Hispanic Arts, 106

Aztec civilization, 46

Aztecs, 47

Baca, Judith Francisca; Baca, Judy,
61, 65

Back-to-Africa Movement, 109

Baker, Josephine, 157

Barraza, Santa, 53

Bedford-Stuyvesant, 31

Bermuda Triangle, 172

Betances, Emeterio, 104

Bhopal, 32

Bible, 93

Black American, 13, 100, 120;
Black community reconstruc-
tion, 95, 97, 99, 101; Black
Power, 14-15, 18, 104

Blauner, Robert, 138, 148

Blourock, Barbara, 148

Bolivia, 60, 63

Bonilla, Frank, 138, 148

Bonnie Prince Charlie, 161

Border Arts Workshop, 57

Boston, 86, 98

Boyz N the Hood, 100

Brazil, 104-105

Britain, 95-96, 98, 100, 161

Brixton, 95-99

Bronx, the, 31, 173

Brown Berets, 104

Budapest, 158

Bull Inter Caetera, 91

Bureau of Indian Affairs, 27

Califas, 55

Campos, Pedro Albizu, 104

Capitalism, 32, 151

Caribbean Cultural Center, 13, 16,
18, 20, 104, 106, 114, 155

Carillo, Graciela, 59

Casely-Hayford, J., 109
Castillo, Consuelo Mendez, 59
Cattaraugus Reservation, 27
Central America, 64, 136; Central
    American, 61
Chalmers, Graeme, 162
Chavez, Cesar, 104
Cherokees, 34
Chicago, 33
Chicana Latina, 59; Chicano
    Movement, 42-44, 47, 58, 66;
    Chicano Park, 55
Christianity, 91, 151, 160
Christmas, 32
Columbus, Christopher, 12, 90, 174
Corridos, 58
Cuba, 104-105
Cultural diversity, 3, 11, 23, 31, 41,
    69, 78-79, 83, 85, 87, 89, 95,
    106, 109, 119, 135-137, 139,
    145, 149, 152, 159, 162, 165,
    170; Cultural equity, 3, 11-12,
    14-15, 31, 37, 39, 75, 78-79, 82,
    95, 100, 107-108, 170; Cultural
    pluralism, 79, 135, 137-143,
    145-149, 152, 168, 170
Cultural Grounding Conference, 3,
    11, 23, 41, 69, 83, 89, 95, 109,
    119, 135, 149, 159, 165;
    Cultural Grounding II
    Conference, 3, 11, 23, 83, 89,
    95, 109, 159, 165
Culture; national and popular, 127-
    131
Cumberland Plateau, 32

DuBois Center, 20
DuBois, W. E. B., 109-110, 113, 115,
    123; Memorial Centre, 113

Eastern Europe, 158, 166, 168
Egypt, 13-14
Einstein, 153
El Plan Espiritual, 66

El Salvador, 63
El Taller Boricua, 104, 106
El Teatro Campesino, 57-58, 66
Emancipation, 16, 116, 151
England, 25, 100, 157, 161
English-speaking Caribbean, 149
Esparza, Phil, 58
Euro-Americans, 91
Eurocentric, 70, 83, 87-88, 104, 130,
    153: Eurocentricity, 162;
    Eurocentrism, 106, 130, 159,
    162

Federalists, 31
First Chicano Youth Liberation
    Conference, 66
Fitzgerald, Ella, 157
Five Nations, 25-26, 91
France, 157, 161
Franklin, Aretha, 157
Franklin, Benjamin, 26
Free Trade Agreement, 63

Galeria de la Raza, 104
Ganondagan, 23
Garibay, Angel, 44
Garvey, Marcus, 17, 109, 115
Garza, Carmen Lomas, 53, 60
Ghana, 20, 109, 113
Ghandi, Mahatma, 62
Goldman, Shifra M., 66
Gomez-Pena, Guillermo, 57, 66
Gordon, Milton, 138, 148
Great Black Music, 130
Great Depression, 121
Great Law of Peace, 90-91
Great Wall Mural Project, 65
Greece, 19
Gringostroika, 173
Gross National Product, 6
Guadalupe Cultural Center, 104
Guadalupe Hidalgo Treaty, 48
Guadalupe-Tonantzin, 53
Guatemala, 63

Hamilton, Alexander, 31
Harding, Vincent, 74, 79, 82
Harlem, 88, 127
Harlem Renaissance, 127
Harvard, 98
Haudenosaunee Confederacy, 25, 89
Helena Film Society, 159
Hernandez, Ester, 60, 65
Hispanic Americans, 23
Hispanic Europeans, 47
Hitler, 91
Hollywood, 166
Home Alone, 6
House of Representatives, 26
Huelga Movement, 57
Hundred Years War, 161
Hungary, 152

Indian Nations, 91-93, 161-162;
         Indian Territory, 24, 34;
         Indian War, 161
Indian-Xicano, 50
Indiana, 148
Inquisition, 160
International Network of Color, 109
Iroquois, 50, 69, 89
Islam, 151, 166
Ixtaccihuatl, 174

Jackson, Jesse, 35
Japan, 86, 158; Japan Foundation,
         86; Japanese American
         National Museum, 84
Jazz, 121, 129-130, 156
Jefferson, Thomas, 31, 35, 62
Jesus, 153
Jews, 91, 153, 157, 160, 162
Johannesburg, 153
Johnson, President Lyndon, 32
Johnson, Samuel, 161
Juice, 100

Kahlo, Frida, 104

Kallen, Horace M., 138, 148
Karenga, Maulana, 125
Keto, C. Tsehloane, 104
King George, 35
King James II, 161
King, Mel, 98
Klor de Alva, J. Jorge, 66
Kongo, 105
Kuralt, Charles, 32
Kurds, 33
Kwanzaa, 125

La Hispaniola, 166
La Nueva Raza, 49-50
La Raza Cosmica, 49
Latin America, 59, 63, 155, 167-168;
         Latin American Indianist
         Movement, 49
Law of Nations, 92
Lazarus, Emma, 6
Lebron, Lolita, 104
Lee County Stockade, 72
Levine, Lawrence, 162
Logan Heights, 55
Los Angeles, 65, 84
Los Toltecas, 55, 57
LUCAC, 47

Madison, James, 26
Marx, Karl, 62
Marxism, 110; Marxists, 110
Mechicanos, 46
Memmi, Albert , 138
Menchu, Rigoberta, 64
Mestizos, 165
Mexican Americans, 50, 57, 63
Middle East, 167
Mission of San Juan Bautista, 58
Mississippi Delta, 31
Mixed-blood Dominicans of Santo
         Domingo, 154
Mohican, 89
Montoya, Jose, 61, 66

Murray, Albert, 5
Museum of Contemporary Hispanic Art, 88
Myrdal, Gunnar, 138

NALAC, 103
Narragansett, 89
Nast, Thomas, 6
National Association of Latino Arts, 103, 106
National Black Arts Festival, 20
National Endowment, 86, 99
Native America, 103
Negritude Movement, 109
Network of Cultural Centers of Color, 106
New York Times, 33; New York University, 86, 138, 148
New York, 3, 11, 14, 23-24, 27, 33, 41, 69, 82-83, 86, 89, 95, 106, 109, 119, 135, 138, 148, 159, 165; New York, City College of, 148; City University of, 138, 148; New York State, 23-24, 27, 89; New York State Office of Parks, 23
New Jack City, 100
Nezahualcoyotl, 46, 50, 51
Nkrumah, Kwame, 110
Noel, Donald L., 146, 148
Non-Christian Values, 144
Noriega, Chon, 47, 66

Ocha, Victor, 55
Okpewho, Isidore, 110
Onondaga, 25-26, 89, 91
Organization of African Unity, 111, 114

Padmore, George, 110
Pantoja, Antonia, 104, 135, 148
Perez, Irene, 59-60
Perot, Ross, 7

Perry, Wilhelmina, 135, 148
Peru, 60, 63
Philadelphia, 26
Pilgrim Fathers, 152
Poole, Marie Louise, 33
Portillo, Miguel Leon, 44, 51
Price, Leontyne, 157
Pueblo Indians, 50
Puerto Rican, 69, 104, 145, 148

Quetzalcoatl, 51-52, 62

Racial oppression, 141, 148; Racism, 33, 60, 62-63, 73, 75-76, 92, 96, 98, 101, 106, 130, 141, 157-158, 163, 170
RCAF (Royal Chicano Airforce), 61
Rio Grande Institute of New Mexico, 61
Roadside Theater, 38
Rodriguez, Patricia, 55, 59-60
Roosevelt, Teddy, 33
Royal Dutch Shell, 32
Rutledge, Samuel, 26

Sacramento, 61, 66
Sahara, 156
San Diego, 55, 169
Santo Domingo, 105, 154
Saudi Arabia, 166
Sebastian, Ellen, 173
Senghor, Leopold Sedar, 110
Sexual preference, 64, 143-145
Shakespeare, 78
Shawnee, 89
Shinnecock, 25
Six Nations Iroquois Confederacy, 89
Sobel, Thomas, 24
Soldier Boy, 58
Sommers, Joseph, 66
South Africa, 32, 136, 153, 156-158
South Bronx, 31

South Carolina, 75
Soviet Union, 158, 166
Soweto, 173
Soyinka, Wole, 113
Spain, 91, 160
Spanish Catholic, 90-91
Spanish Crown, 92; Spanish
     Europe, 103
Statue of Liberty, 6
Steinberg, Stephen, 161
Summit of African Heads of State,
     114
Susquehanna, 36

Tainos, 105
Tecumseh, 89
Temple University, 13, 104
Thatcher, Margaret, 153
Thomas, Clarence, 21
Torres, Salvador Roberto, 55
Toynbee, Arnold, 33
Tubman, Harriet, 72, 77
Tuchman, Barbara, 160
Turtle Island, 24
Tuscarora Nation, 25
Tze, Chuang, 8

U. S. Census, 47
U. S. Constitution, 93
UNESCO, 108
Union Carbide, 32
United Colors of Benetton, 170
United Farmworkers, 57
United League of Latin Americans,
     47
United Mine Workers of America-
     Pittston, 34
United Nations, 92, 113-114, 167;
     United Nations Charter, 114
United States Department of Labor,
     136, 148
United States Supreme Court, 93
University of California, 60

University of Nigeria, 110

Valdez, Luis, 62
Vallejo, Linda, 60
Vasconcellos, Jose, 49
Vega, Bernardo, 105
Venezuela, 60, 105
Villa, Pancho, 104
Virginia, 32-33

Wales, 161
Wampum, 25-26
War of Spanish Secession, 161
Warsaw, 158
Washington Redskins, 25
West Africa, 151, 153; West African,
     122, 130
West Indians, 151
West Virginia, 32; West Virginia-
     Pike County, 32
Western Europe, 40, 160-161, 168;
     Western European, 70-71, 83,
     159, 165
Whitney Museum of American Art,
     66, 85

Xiaotung, Fei, 4
Xicana, 61; Xicano Amerindian, 50,
     54, 57; Xicano Movement, 50-
     51, 56-59, 65; Xicano, the, 46-
     54, 56-59, 61-62, 64-65;
     Xicano-Indian, 49-50

Yankee, 6, 56
Yaqui, 50, 60
Ybarra-Frausto, Tomas, 56, 66
Yellow Creek, Kentucky, 38

Zalazar, Reuben, 104
Zapata, Emiliano, 104
Zhuangtzu, 8
Zoot Suit, 58